THE BOOK OF
PILATES

THE BOOK OF
PILATES

Bath · New York · Singapore · Hong Kong · Cologne · Delhi · Melbourne

This edition published by Parragon in 2010

Parragon
Queen Street House
4 Queen Street
Bath BA1 1HE, UK

ISBN: 978-1-4454-0838-5

Printed in China

Designed and created by Bridgewater Book Company Limited
Cover by 20 Twenty Design.

NOTE
As a precautionary measure, the publishers advise that anyone intending to follow
the exercise programs outlined in this book should first consult a qualified medical
practitioner or therapist.

Cover images (l-r)
Girl does Pilates © iStock
Woman doing exercise © iStock
Young woman making lotus position © IMAGEMORE Co, Ltd/Getty Images

contents

introduction

introduction

The Pilates technique was developed in the early years of the 20th century by a young German who was determined to overcome his physical disabilities and become a fit and healthy individual. His efforts were totally successful, and his methods are not only still used today, but are growing in popularity as the benefits of this gentle form of exercise are recognised.

The technique, consisting of a series of controlled, flowing movements, will not only improve your shape but will also promote flexibility, remedy any postural problems you may have by realigning your body structure to its natural balance, and allow internal organs to function more efficiently. The primary aim of the exercises is to promote stability in the 'core' or 'centre' of the body – that is, the area around your middle where the muscles that support the spine are located – and in the shoulder girdle and pelvis.

This is not frenetic aerobic exercise, to be carried out mechanically to the thumping rhythm of deafening music – the Pilates system is underpinned by focused concentration and conscious flowing breath. Each movement is carried out with balance and precision, and you maintain a constant connection between mind and body, feeding information between the two. Pilates is a truly holistic approach to physical and mental health and harmony.

Does this sound too good to be true? Are you wondering where the catch is? Well, there isn't one – the only thing you need to bear in mind is that Pilates is not a 'quick fix'. It takes time and can be tough, especially if you are starting from a position where your muscle tone and posture are very poor. But as long as you understand and adhere to the principles and techniques, keep a steady rhythm, and follow the instructions to the letter, the rewards will be great – you will both look and feel fantastic, and be brimming with a new vitality and confidence. Just remember to think tortoise, not hare!

Below

The aim of the Pilates technique is to carry out the sequence of movements in a controlled, flowing way, maintaining a constant connection between mind and body.

How to use this book

It is essential that you understand the principles of Pilates before you start practising the movements, so it is suggested that you read through the whole book at least once, and then go back and familiarise yourself thoroughly with the techniques explained in the Body and Mind chapter. Work through the exercises in this section to help you master these techniques.

You will then be ready to move on to the Warm-Ups and Introductory Level Exercises. It is suggested that you practise at that level at least twice a week for about six to eight weeks, working to gain stability of the central core and control of the deep abdominal and postural muscles. Once you feel confident, go on to the Beginner Level Exercises, again keeping stability in mind. When you are very familiar with the techniques, you can progress on to the ultimate challenge – the advanced level moves.

Some of the exercises are basically the same, with just a little extra challenge as you move up a level to help you progress – if you are unsure of a move, go back to the previous level until you feel ready to move on.

Although Pilates is a very safe and gentle form of exercise, it is strongly advised that you take the precaution of obtaining medical clearance from your doctor before you start.

STEP-BY-STEP SPREADS

Introduction
This section outlines the aim of the exercise and the areas it benefits, and includes useful tips, advice and information.

Instructions
The step-by-step instructions are a clear, detailed guide to achieving the sequence of movements.

Illustrations
The photographs support the step-by-step instructions to help you achieve the correct movement and position.

Variations
Some exercises include modifications or progressions to the basic step-by-step instructions.

the history of pilates

Joseph H. Pilates was born in Düsseldorf in Germany in 1880. As a young child he suffered from a number of debilitating ailments, including asthma and rickets, which at that time would normally have left him severely crippled, if not permanently bedridden. But Pilates was blessed with a very positive attitude and, although he was so young, he was determined not to let his physical disabilities take over his life.

He began to study various methods of exercise and body-building, but instead of concentrating on just one or two of these, he took the elements he required from all of them and developed his own method – which he later called 'Contrology' – with great success. By his early teens, Pilates had grown into a fit and healthy individual, and he went on to become an enthusiastic sportsman, excelling in skiing, diving, gymnastics and boxing. He could even include circus performer among his extraordinary list of achievements! Then, at the age of 32, he moved to England, where he became a professional boxer and taught self-defence to detectives at the police headquarters at Scotland Yard.

When the First World War broke out two years later, Pilates was interned by the British authorities as a German national. He made constructive use of his time to develop his interest in creating and maintaining an optimum state of health, and the Pilates system was born of the belief that true well-being is achieved through a combination of physical fitness and a positive mental attitude. He shared his beliefs with his fellow internees, who were said to have remained exceptionally healthy as a result! He also set many seriously injured internees on the road to rehabilitation, helping them regain muscle tone by attaching springs to their beds to provide resistance as they carried out gentle exercise movements.

After the war Pilates returned to Germany for a few years, where he worked with other pioneers of the movement technique. In 1926 he set sail for New York, and on the way met his future wife, Clara, who shared his radical views on health and fitness. The couple set up an exercise studio together, and soon met with growing success among people from a variety of disciplines. Pilates' method appealed particularly to dancers, actors, athletes and gymnasts, who were keen to gain strength, vitality, stamina and grace, but not the bulky muscles that went hand-in-hand with some body-building techniques. What Pilates taught them was an holistic approach to health – his philosophy embraced total commitment to regular practice of the exercises, a diet that promoted physical and mental fitness, and that all-important attitude of determination and motivation.

Pilates also helped clients suffering from injuries to a speedy recovery by making an immediate start on their rehabilitation. He designed a piece of equipment based on the experiments he had carried out with injured internees during the war – a sliding bed with springs that could be adjusted to suit the patient's stage of recovery. Equipment based on this concept is used today in many modern Pilates studios.

Pilates may have started life as a weak, frail, sickly individual, but against all odds he recovered and remained healthy until his death at the age of 87, a shining example of the effectiveness of his approach to fitness. He wrote several books on the subject, including *Your Health* (published 1934) and *Return to Life through Contrology* (1945). Nothing escaped his notice in his quest for optimum health – it is not by chance that several of the movements are reminiscent of a cat stretching!

The 'true' Pilates method was never formally taught or documented, and indeed Pilates himself varied his method of teaching the exercises to meet the individual needs of his clients. This means that over the years practitioners have developed their own variations and methods of teaching the system – but they are all based on Pilates' excellent and enduring principles.

Below
The Pilates system takes elements from many sources, including the way in which a cat bends and stretches.

body and mind

vital techniques

"We live in a modern society that loves shortcut techniques. Yet, quality of life cannot be achieved by taking the right shortcut. There is no shortcut, but there is a path. The path is based on principles revered throughout history. If there is one message to glean from this wisdom, it is that a meaningful life is not a matter of speed or efficiency. It's much more a matter of what you do and why you do it, than how fast you get it done."

Stephen R. Covey, *First Things*

When Stephen Covey wrote this passage, he was talking about the organization and management of time—but his principles are appropriate to many things in life, including practice of the Pilates system. Pilates is a path toward a healthy body that functions at maximum efficiency. If you follow the path at the prescribed speed, adhering to the principles and techniques involved, you will get the result you want. If you try to stray from the path, hoping for a quicker result, you are likely to fail. So be patient, and learn to enjoy your steady progress. It may seem an impossible task at first, but it will be worth it!

There are many different exercises, ranging from warm-up exercises and beginners' exercises to advanced level exercises; but the basic principles and techniques of Pilates are common to all levels, and are vital to the success of the exercises. To begin with, it is important that you take a little time to read through the following pages, and practice the exercises for breathing and abdominal hollowing—do not start practicing the Pilates movements, even at the warm-up level, until you are confident that you have mastered these basic techniques.

Breathing

Breathing is something we do naturally and instinctively, without thinking, and we take it for granted that the way we breathe is the right way. Very often, however, our breathing is shallow, and we fail to take in sufficient air to oxygenate the blood properly. This in turn leaves us feeling tired and lethargic, adversely affecting both our energy levels and our spirits.

Controlled and effective breathing is vital to the Pilates technique, and mastering the art of breathing correctly is perhaps the steepest of the Pilates learning curves. Disciplines such as martial arts, tai chi, and yoga emphasize the importance of conscious breathing to help calm and focus the mind, release physical tension, and enhance learning—and Pilates is no exception.

To check whether you breathe properly, lie down on the floor, breathe in through your nose, and observe where that breath is going. If all that happens is that your upper chest moves a little, and then you exhale, your breathing is not effective. If you take a deep breath, pulling in your stomach tightly, then exhale and let everything go, your breathing is still not effective—in either of these cases,

you will need to re-educate yourself.

The Pilates breath is wide and full into your back and sides, filling the lungs like bellows, expanding the diaphragm and pushing your ribcage out to the sides—imagine a bucket handle being lifted out. When you exhale, the diaphragm contracts, pushing all the stale air out of the lungs. Each step in the Pilates exercises begins with a direction to inhale or exhale, and the movement accompanies the breath. You must have proper control over your breathing, so that the breath comes and goes in a steady, rhythmic, flowing way—otherwise, you will very likely find yourself holding your breath as you rush through the movement before collapsing in a breathless heap!

Centering

All movement comes from a strong, central "core"—the area below the base of the ribcage and above the line across the hip-bones. Here, the transversus abdominus and the lumbar multifidus muscles together form an invisible "girdle of strength" around the body, which Pilates referred to as the "powerhouse." If you have poor posture or a bad back, this is an indication that your center is weak. The first aim of Pilates exercises is to strengthen this area by conditioning and toning the muscles to promote easy, flowing movement and good posture.

Control and concentration

"Good posture can be successfully acquired only when the entire mechanism of the body is under perfect control."
J.H. Pilates

Mental and physical fitness is the result of a constant exchange of information and feedback between mind and body. While you are training, be focused on what you are doing—still your mind and let it listen to your body, and be aware of all sensations. Concentrate fully on each move so that you bring mind and body together to create a pattern of balanced and controlled movements, each one flowing slowly, gently, and gracefully into the next.

Precision

"The benefits of Pilates depend solely on your performing the exercises exactly according to the instructions."
J.H. Pilates

Don't be tempted to do your own thing. Read the directions carefully for each movement, and make sure you understand them before practicing the move. Carry out each move with precision—focus your attention on the relevant area of the body, make sure you are breathing fully and deeply, and inhale and exhale at the correct point in the exercise.

Rushing through each movement and increasing the number of repetitions will not make it more effective—in Pilates, quality is far more important than quantity.

Relaxation and alignment

Before starting your Pilates session, take a few minutes to relax your mind and body. It's important that your body is correctly aligned to enable you to carry out the movements in a natural, flowing way with ease and precision. Before you start any movement—whether you are standing, sitting, or lying face up or down— make sure:

• Your head is in alignment with your body and not tilted to one side or the other.
• Your shoulders are in line with your hips—imagine that your shoulder blades are sliding or "melting" down your back.
• Your knees are in line with your hips.
• Your feet are in line with your knees.
• Your back (see page18) and pelvis (see page 29) are in "neutral."

Motivation and visualization

Adopting and maintaining a positive mental attitude are key elements in the success of any new venture—without his positive outlook, Pilates would not have achieved his goal. It is a daunting prospect to make changes in your life, although you know they will be of benefit to you, and it's all too easy to give up before you even start. Phrases such as, "I can't do that," or "It's too late to change now," are unhelpful—so just don't use them! Instead, say firmly to yourself, "Yes, I can do that and I will succeed." Say it every day! You may feel silly at first, but you'll really appreciate it when the results of your efforts start to become visible to you. Before you start practicing the Pilates technique, fix a clear picture in your mind of what you want to achieve. It may be that you simply want to look and feel your best—long, lean, graceful, and brimming with self-confidence—or you may have physical problems that you wish to overcome, such as a bad back. Either way, Pilates is there to help you— as long as you let it.

anatomy: bones

One of the main aims of Pilates is to bring the skeletal system back to its natural alignment. The key points of the skeleton that are involved are the spine, the shoulder girdle, and the pelvis, which are all essential to maintaining good posture. Pilates also mobilizes the joints, and can help increase bone density, reducing the risk of osteoporosis and its associated problems, such as fractures.

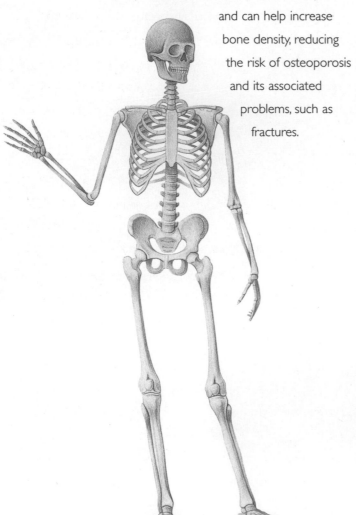

Pilates helps maintain a healthy skeletal system.

The spine

The spine is made up of 34 separate bones, called vertebrae. These form a column to protect the delicate spinal cord, a key part of the nervous system that delivers messages throughout the body from the brain, and returns messages from the body to the brain. The spine also connects and supports the rest of the skeleton.

Viewed from behind, the spine appears to be straight from top to bottom, but if you look at it in profile, you will see that it has four natural curves, which act as shock absorbers during movement. A number of the Pilates exercises instruct you to ensure that your spine is in "neutral." This means that you let your spine rest in its natural curves. If you are standing up, you should neither stretch out the spine unnaturally, nor slump so that the curves are exaggerated. When you are lying down, do not press your back down into the floor or arch it so that the lower back comes up off the floor. Simply relax, so that your spine falls into its natural, "neutral" position.

When doing Pilates, you are also often asked to roll or unroll the back, one vertebra at a time. The vertebrae are joined together by ligaments, and cartilage disks between each vertebra prevent friction. This segmented, protected structure enables you to roll and unroll in a controlled, flowing way.

The shoulder girdle

The arms are joined to the torso at the shoulders. Three bones are attached to each shoulder—the clavicle, or collar bone, which is also joined to the top of the breastbone; the scapula, or shoulder blade; and the humerus, or upper arm bone. There is plenty of scope for bad posture stemming from the shoulders. We are often told to "stand up straight," but this may encourage you to pull your shoulders too far back into an unnatural position, causing strain across the collar bone and upper ribcage. You may habitually sit slumped forward, perhaps because your desk and chair are the wrong height, causing strain across the back or your shoulders may have become unbalanced as a result of carrying heavy shopping. Tension is often carried in the shoulders, causing them to hunch up toward your ears. Finding the correct position for your shoulders is essential to creating good posture and correcting back pain.

The pelvis

The pelvis is joined to the lower part of the spine, and the legs are attached to the pelvis at the hip joints. A misaligned pelvis is another common problem, which can be caused by an unbalanced sitting position, for example, or by holding a baby propped on a hip. The abdominal muscles, which form part of the central "core," are attached to the pelvis at the pubic bone. Putting the pelvis into "neutral" means neither pushing it back (so that your bottom sticks out and your lower spine curves unnaturally), nor pushing it forward, (so that your stomach sticks out and your spine is straightened). Again, the pelvis should be allowed to fall into its natural, neutral position so that it doesn't cause strain elsewhere.

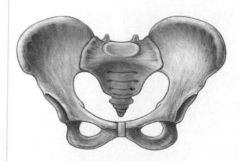

A correctly aligned pelvis is essential to maintaining good posture.

anatomy: muscles

Muscles are tissues that work together in pairs to create movement—as one muscle contracts, the other relaxes. To help you visualize this in action, hold out your arm in front of you with your hand palm down and fingers pointing forward, parallel to the floor. Now let your hand flop down at the wrist—you can see how the muscles on the upper side of

the wrist relax and stretch to let the muscles on the under side of the wrist contract. The more you pull your fingers back toward the under side of your wrist, the more the upper muscles have to stretch and the tighter the lower muscles become to let the movement take place.

Muscles need to be used regularly to keep them strong, and also stretched regularly to keep them flexible. Unfortunately, the modern inclination to travel everywhere by car instead of walking, coupled with the necessity to spend long hours sitting at a desk, means that many people do not give their muscles the attention they need to stay healthy. When muscles are not used very much, they become weak and lose elasticity, making movement more difficult—if you have ever had an illness that has kept you in bed even for just a few days, you will know how weak and wobbly you feel when you first get up and start to move

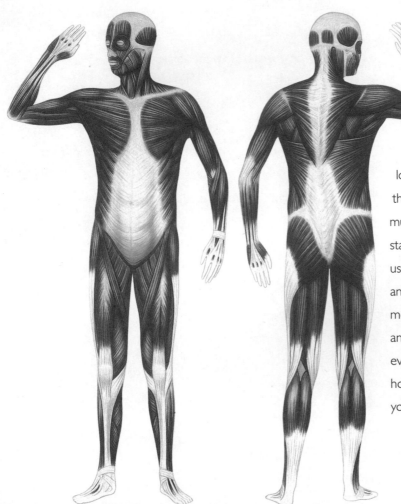

Strengthening the body's musculature to enhance support of the skeletal system is one of the main aims of Pilates, leading to greatly improved posture.

about again. Pilates recognized that prolonged lack of use, following major illness or serious injury, led to the physical infirmity he suffered as a child, and he was a great believer in starting rehabilitation as early as possible to avoid unnecessary muscle wastage. (If you are recovering from a major illness or injury, you should always consult your doctor and a registered Pilates practitioner to advise you on a program of rehabilitation.)

Muscles are at their most powerful and effective when they are well-toned but also relaxed. If your muscles have either become very tense (overcontracted) or are completely lacking in tone (overstretched), any movement can quickly lead to injury. An overcontracted muscle will stay tight even when you are not moving, and movement from an overcontracted muscle can lead to wear and tear on a joint as it tries to compensate by pulling toward the muscle. A weak, overstretched muscle can lead to instability around a joint, resulting in slow reflex actions. Pilates exercises aim to tone the muscles so that they are strong but flexible, enabling all movement to start from a state of relaxation.

The most important muscles targeted by the Pilates technique are those that form the "girdle of strength"—primarily the deep postural transversus abdominus and lumbar multifidus, supported by the pelvic floor muscles. If your abdominal muscles are very weak, you will need to devote some time to strengthening them, or you may find other, stronger muscle groups trying to take over the work. It is very tempting, for example, to engage the gluteus maximus—the buttocks—instead of the pelvic floor muscles, especially as you are more likely to be able to feel the contraction, or to try and flex the upper body by lifting the head and shoulders and tensing the muscles in the upper back. Once the abdominal muscles are strengthened and toned, however, all movement will become easier and more fluid, and you can then concentrate on working on muscle groups elsewhere, confident that you are supported by a strong center.

posture

"Good posture can be successfully acquired only when the entire mechanism of the body is under perfect control."
J.H. Pilates

There is a lot to be said for achieving and maintaining good posture. On a purely esthetic level, people with good posture look taller, sleeker, and more graceful than those who slouch along or slump in a chair, looking as if they are thoroughly fed up with life or trying very hard not to be noticed! Good posture automatically makes you feel more confident, too, and you will radiate this confidence to the world. "Walk tall" is a very sound piece of advice!

On a physical level, we expect an awful lot from our bodies. Evolution has led us to move in an upright position, defying gravity, and if we don't take care of our posture, gravity will eventually start to defy us. Added to this, we often spend hours at a time sitting down at our desks or driving; we wedge the phone between ear and shoulder so that we can carry on working as we talk; we carry heavy bags or briefcases, often favoring one side of the body—we really ask for trouble!

Poor posture can contribute to any number of ailments. Perhaps the most obvious of these is back pain—you will be far less prone to this debilitating complaint if you don't put unnecessary strain on the muscles through sloppy posture. But have you ever made the connection between poor posture and shortness of breath or irritable bowel syndrome? Adopting the correct posture allows your internal organs to work at their optimum levels—for example, your breathing will be more efficient if your lung capacity isn't restricted by your ribcage, and you are less likely to suffer from digestive problems if your stomach and intestines aren't compressed.

If you suspect your posture is less than perfect, stand in front of a full-length mirror and take a good look at yourself. Your shoulders should be level, and there should be an equal distance between your ears and shoulders—this shows that you are not pulling your body out of balance by tilting your head to left or right. Your hips should be level, and also your kneecaps—if your weight isn't evenly distributed, there will be a joint or muscle somewhere in your body that is over-burdened, even if only very slightly.

Now stand sideways to the mirror. Your head should be centered over your body and your spine should be erect but relaxed. Common postural problems include an exaggerated arch in the lower back, which throws the abdomen forward, or a slouch, which forces the head to fall forward, shortening the neck at the front and compressing the chest and abdomen.

Be honest! If you have inspected yourself in the mirror and you seem to be looking pretty good – then you relax and your posture collapses completely, you need to do some work on yourself! If you were cheating, your first instinct was probably to pull in your stomach, which automatically made you tuck in your tail, straighten your spine and your head, and bring your shoulders into line with your ears. In other words, you pulled everything into correct alignment. When you relaxed, you probably did so by letting the stomach go—and everything else followed. When you strengthen the abdomen through Pilates, holding in your stomach will cease to be an effort, and even when you relax completely, you will still retain good posture.

Long hours spent working at a computer can lead to postural problems.

Good posture should be maintained even when you are completely relaxed.

breathing

We have already seen that correct and effective breathing is essential to practicing Pilates—so take some time to learn the breathing technique. You are aiming for a gentle, non-exaggerated breath, and to breathe laterally, encouraging the ribcage to move out to the sides and back. The movement of the ribcage is described as "pail handle"—as you inhale, the ribs move up and out, as if a pail handle were being lifted, and as you exhale, the ribs move back to the center and slightly down, as if the pail handle were being replaced.

Go through the following exercise step by step, using your hands to give you feedback.

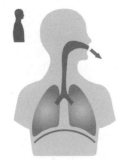 

Left
If you are breathing correctly, the chest and diaphragm should expand as you inhale, filling the lungs, and contract as you exhale, pushing the air out of the body.

1 STEP ONE
Find a warm, comfortable space and sit down on the floor. You will be here for a while, so you might like to sit on a cushion or a mat.

2 STEP TWO
Sit upright, with your shoulders relaxed and your legs crossed. Place one hand on your chest and another on your stomach, around the navel area.

3 STEP THREE
Close your eyes and for a moment inhale and exhale, as you would normally. Gently press your hands against your body, and feel the movement of your body as you breathe. You may feel your chest rise a little, and your stomach move in and out, or you may feel nothing at all.

STEP FOUR

4

Now change your hand position. Close together the fingers and thumb of both hands, as if you were going to make a chopping movement. Place the heel of each hand on the side of the ribcage, with the fingers extended to the soft opening at the center. Relax your shoulders and let the shoulder blades melt down your back.

VARIATIONS

Try the same technique standing up, lying on your back or face down, or in the crook position (sitting up with your knees bent at 45 degrees, feet flat on the floor). It will be easier to find the connection in some positions than in others, but you should still try them all in preparation for carrying out the exercises.

STEP FIVE

5

Making sure there is no tension in the body, inhale through the nose and exhale with a sigh through a relaxed open jaw: remember the "H" sound in "hollow." Breathe in an even rhythm—try inhaling to a mental count of four and exhaling to a mental count of four. Maintain the relaxed position of your shoulders.

STEP SIX

6

Now close your eyes, and sense within your body how you are feeling. You should be sitting comfortably, with your hands on the ribcage, shoulders relaxed and the breathing flowing to a gentle rhythm.

STEP SEVEN

7

With the heels of your hands, apply gentle pressure to the ribcage—make your mind and body aware of the area. Inhale gently as if breathing to the heels of your hands, feeling your ribcage expand to the sides; as you exhale, feel the ribs closing into the center. Repeat for nine more breaths. Get a sense of the flow—feel the "pail handle" move out and up, in and down.

body placement and muscle synergy

Core conditioning

Pilates is a synergistic activity, and this means that for each individual movement in each exercise—whether you are working at the most basic or the most advanced level—every part of the body is working together to bring about the desired result. As we have already seen, the first priority with Pilates is to create the strong, stable "center" or "core"—which Pilates referred to as the dynamic "girdle of strength" or "powerhouse"—from which stems perfect posture as well as all movement in the body. When you are practicing the Pilates technique, you will frequently come across the direction to "maintain the connection with the center," and until you can do this with

Left and opposite
Before practicing the Pilates technique, you must learn how to locate and correctly activate the transversus abdominus muscle.

complete ease and without effort, you will not be able to focus all your attention on the area you are working. So what is this all-important center, and where do you find it? Well, loosely speaking it is the area located between an imaginary line running around the body just below the diaphragm and another running above the pelvic floor. It is three muscles found within this area that are engaged to create a strong center. These are the muscles that stabilize the lower spine in the lumbar region of the back, and they are positioned very deep and close to the spine itself—the transversus abdominus to the front of the spine and the lumbar multifidus to the back, both in line with the navel, and the pelvic floor muscles at the base.

The transversus abdominus is one of the four muscles that make up the abdominal wall, and is the deepest of the four. To help you locate the position of this muscle, stand up so that you are straight but relaxed, take both hands and grab your sides with your thumbs around your waist pointing toward your back, and your fingers pointing in toward the navel.

When you have a firm hold, give a good cough! As you cough, you will feel a muscle bounce beneath your fingers. Now take a breath in, and then blow out—you will feel the same muscle bounce again. This is the transversus abdominus (TVA) and, because it is such a vital component in core stability, it is essential to learn how to engage it properly.

TVA activation

As with everything, there is a right way and a wrong way to go about activating the TVA. Let's start with the wrong way, which is simply to overdo it by sucking in your abdomen with such gusto that it's almost sticking to your spine. What you are aiming for is to master a gentle contraction of the TVA—one that you can maintain easily at all times, whether you are standing still, walking, or exercising or sitting and either working at a desk or relaxing in your favorite comfortable chair.

To understand the reason for this, you need to know that there are two types of muscle—mobilizers (task muscles) and stabilizers (postural muscles). Muscles that mobilize are responsible for large movements, such as kicking or throwing—they mobilize limbs. Compared to stabilizers, they are superficial (closer to the surface), longer, work harder (at approximately 40–100% of their power) and are phasic—i.e., they tire quickly, so work in phases for short periods, turning on and off.

Muscles that stabilize are close to the spine or lie deeply; they are shorter than mobilizers, work for longer periods, and are tonic (i.e., they hold tone). Stabilisers need endurance and so they work at only about 20–30% of their maximum voluntary contraction (MVC). The TVA is a stabilizer muscle—a deep, postural muscle—so this is why it is important to work it gently.

Working the TVA

How do you recognize when you are working at the correct level of TVA contraction—30%? Read this exercise through, then try it out.

Stand up, keeping good posture in mind—stand tall, with your knees slightly kinked, but not locked, your tail bone pointing toward the floor, and your shoulders relaxed, as though your shoulder blades were melting down your back towards your pelvis. Hold your head upright, so that your ears point toward the ceiling, and focus your eyes on the horizon. In this position, you will feel elongated—stretched from head to toe. Now let your stomach relax as far as it will go—and give this position a score of 0%. Return to the first position.

Now pull everything in so that your whole body feels sucked in and tense—pull your stomach into your spine and elevate your shoulders until they are almost touching your ears. You should now bear a strong resemblance to Frankenstein! Give this position a score of 100%, so the yardstick is 0% for no tone and 100% for tense to the point of being unable to breath.

To get to 30%, return to the first position again, standing tall but relaxed. Take your right hand and place your thumb at the lower edge of your navel, then splay your fingers and span your hand until the little finger is toward the pubic bone, resting your hand on your stomach. Draw your navel in and up toward your spine, away from your hand, to 100%, then release it halfway to 50% while retaining your elongated stance—do not slump. Now release a little farther, and you have reached 30%—you should have a sensation of feeling connected but not tense, in a position that you can maintain all day and every day, whatever you are doing.

Engaging the pelvic floor

The pelvic floor muscles are an important element in stabilizing the spine, working in conjunction with the TVA. A gentle contraction is sufficient to activate the pelvic floor—do not be tempted to clench the buttocks in an effort to feel the tension. Lie on your back and place your hand on the lower abdominal area, then gently exhale, and draw up the muscles from below and in front of the pelvic area—as you do so, you will feel the TVA contracting.

Neutral pelvis

The pelvis is the base of support for the body—your spine rests upon it and your legs move from it, so for optimum movement the pelvis should be "organized" in the best possible postural position. This position is described as "neutral."

To help you identify the perfect position, lie on your back with your knees bent to 45 degrees, your feet flat on the floor, and your body relaxed. Place your hands in a triangle over your stomach, with your thumbs forming the base of the triangle at the navel, and your fingers splaying toward the pubic bone to form the point. When the pelvis is properly organized, your palms should be flat on your lower stomach muscles, and your hip-bones should be positioned evenly on either side of your hands. If your fingers are raised higher than your thumbs, your pelvis is in a posterior tilt, and if your thumbs are higher than your fingers, it is because your pelvis is in an anterior tilt. When your pelvis is in neutral, your hands will be absolutely level, with your spine neither too flat to the floor nor arched to the ceiling. The "Neutral to Imprinted Spine (50/50)" exercise on page 64 helps you to settle into this position.

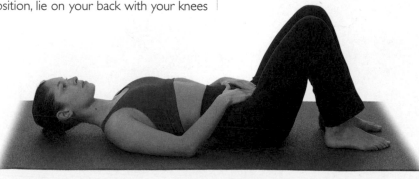

Abdominal hollowing

Abdominal hollowing is created when the deep postural abdominal muscles are contracted, and is the result of correct breathing. As we have already seen, it is essential to inhale and exhale gently, and not try to force the breath. As you inhale, you should get a sense of the ribs moving to the sides and the back, not up and away. As you exhale, drawing the navel in and up toward the spine, you should get a sense of the ribs closing in and moving toward the hips as if on railroad tracks. If you force the breath out, you will engage the external oblique muscles and end up with a bulging, dome-shaped abdomen—not what you want at all!
Practice with the following exercise.

1 STEP ONE
Stand or sit comfortably and elongate the spine, lengthening through the crown of your head to the ceiling, and through your tail bone to the floor.

2 STEP TWO
Shrug your shoulders to your ears, then roll gently backward, letting your shoulder blades glide down your back toward your pelvis.

3 STEP THREE
With your shoulders relaxed, place one hand on either side of your ribcage, with your fingertips facing each other at the opening between the ribcage. Inhale gently, and feel your ribcage moving gently out toward the sides.

4 STEP FOUR
Exhale gently, relaxing the jaw and sighing softly through an open mouth. Draw up on the pelvic floor and back on the navel toward the spine to a maximum of 30%, as described earlier, feeling the ribs move in toward the center and gently downward, creating the hollow—a "slope" from the ribs to the pelvis. If you exhale to the "H" sound of "hollow," it will open the mouth and drop the jaw, helping you resist the temptation to either blow out or force the exhale through pursed lips.

Lengthening the neck

All Pilates movements are geared toward realigning the body into a perfect posture, with the spine in optimum alignment. The neck—the top of the spine, or "cervical spine"—is a very important part of this process.

Maintaining correct alignment in the neck is particularly important when you are flexing the upper body off the floor. It's tempting to lift with the shoulders and head, jamming the chin into the chest or, even worse, hanging the head backward like a hinged coffeepot lid.

To lengthen the neck in preparation for flexing the upper body correctly from a strong central core, rock the chin SLIGHTLY toward the chest, without lifting your head—you should feel as if someone has taken your head in both hands and gently stretched it away from your shoulders. Your neck will now remain in alignment.

The gaze

When you walk along gazing at the floor, your head is downcast and your posture slumped forward—but look up and focus your gaze on the horizon, and you will stand tall and upright, with your head and neck in alignment with your spine. Perfect!

Directing your gaze at the horizon when you are carrying out the Pilates movements will help the movement flow as well as helping you maintain alignment. If you are doing a sit-up, for example, and you keep your gaze on the ceiling, your head will fall back, compressing your neck and spine. If you let your gaze follow the horizon as you move, however, so that it is focused in front of you at knee level when you reach the top of the movement, your head and neck will be aligned and in the optimum position. This is a good example of the synergistic nature of Pilates—you will find it progressively easier to direct your gaze correctly as your center becomes stronger and more stable. Your center will become stronger when you let it do its work and do not inadvertently substitute other muscle groups by directing your gaze incorrectly.

visualization and feedback

Visualisation

"When we create something, we always create it first in a thought form. A thought or idea always precedes manifestation. ... Imagination is the ability to create an idea or mental picture in your mind. In creative visualization, you use your imagination to create a clear image of something to manifest. Then you continue to focus on the idea."

Shakti Gawain, Creative Visualization

To visualize something is to create a picture of the desired outcome in your mind's eye and to hold it there as a constant source of inspiration and motivation. If this sounds unrealistic to you, think about how often you visualize things without realizing that this is what you are doing. For instance, you take a look around your living-room, which is looking a bit old and tired. You hate that flowery wallpaper, and would love to replace it with plain painted walls. Two new sofas would look great instead of the old three-piece suite. That clutter needs sorting, and the things you want to keep could be stored away neatly instead of piling up in the corners. Some new drapes and a huge vase of fresh flowers instead of that dusty, withered old houseplant would complete the look. You see? You've created a clear image in your mind of a change you would like to make! Now you continue to focus on the idea until your revamped living-room is completed.

So why not try the same technique on yourself, and visualise a new you? Take a look at the jaded old you, with all your aches and pains and stresses reflected in your face and posture. Now visualize the new you—upright and confident, sleek and streamlined, free from stress and ailments, glowing with health and vitality. Sounds good? Well, it worked for Joseph Pilates and it can work for you. Just hold the image in your mind, and focus on it as you are working with Pilates' technique. You can keep your goal in mind by hanging your favorite—but perhaps, at the moment, rather too tight?—outfit where you can see it as you exercise, and visualize yourself fitting into it and looking better than ever before. Or try taking a photograph before you start, then take more at regular intervals so that you can see how well you have progressed—a visual source of motivation!

Biofeedback and body awareness

Biofeedback is a tool that will assist the mind-body connection. Most of us move around on automatic pilot, unaware of how it should feel to connect or contract a muscle correctly.

To raise your awareness of how one movement affects another part of the body, try lying flat on the floor with your hands resting on your stomach in a triangle shape. The thumbs form the base of the triangle at the navel, and the fingers splay down to form a point at the pubic bone. Now imagine you have a glass of water balanced on the triangle and you are trying not to spill it. Focus all your attention on drawing the navel back toward the spine in a gentle, controlled movement. You will feel the movement beneath your hands, but be conscious of what is happening to the pelvis and hips—unless they remain balanced and stable, that imaginary glass of water will spill everywhere!

When carrying out your Pilates exercises, keep that mind-body connection open all the time, giving and receiving constant feedback about the part of the body you are working on and how each movement affects the rest of the body.

before you start

Environment

It is essential to find a quiet, comfortable place for your Pilates session, where you will not be disturbed. If you can allocate some time when you are alone at home, this is ideal—unplug the telephone, ignore the doorbell, and focus all your attention on yourself. If there are usually other family members at home when you are, be firm about claiming some time for yourself—it's easier to do this if you can schedule in a regular time. Make sure the room you work in is warm but well-ventilated, and that you have plenty of space to lie down with your arms outstretched.

You will not need any special equipment, but working on a padded exercise mat, a rug, or a folded blanket is essential to protect your spine from bruising. A full-length mirror is also useful, so that you can keep a constant check on your position—what you think you are doing and what you are actually doing may not be the same!

Clothing

Choose light, comfortable clothing that lets you move without restriction—fairly close-fitting leggings or cycling shorts, with a T-shirt or leotard top, are ideal because they are totally flexible and will move with you. It's best to exercise in your bare feet, but you can wear socks if you prefer.

Below

Choose light, comfortable clothing and go barefoot to give unrestricted movement when you are carrying out the Pilates exercises.

When to exercise ...

Pilates exercises can be done at any time, and there are advantages to both ends of the day. In the morning Pilates can be energizing, especially if you normally find it difficult to come alive then, while in the evening it is useful for unwinding—it is really a matter of personal preference and knowing when you are most likely to get some quiet time for yourself.

If you choose the morning, make sure you warm up sufficiently before you start as your muscles will not have had a chance to get mobilized, and ensure that you have enough time to focus on what you are doing—you will not be able to concentrate fully otherwise.

... and when not to exercise

Do not exercise if you are feeling at all unwell, or have not fully recovered from a recent illness. You must also avoid exercise after eating a heavy meal or drinking alcohol, or if you are taking pain-killers—whether over-the-counter or prescribed—as these will mask any warning signs of injury.

It is important that you are neither cold nor stressed when you start exercising. Deep breathing for a few minutes is an excellent way to de-stress—find a quiet, comfortable place to do this, and imagine that you are releasing your stresses as you exhale, and taking in peace as you inhale.

Walking on the spot for a few minutes, or taking a short, brisk walk outside in good weather, will help release both mental and physical tension. It will also warm you up at the same time by getting your circulation going—if you start exercising when your joints and muscles are chilled, you are far more likely to injure yourself. Don't be tempted to warm yourself up by taking a hot bath, as this will relax your muscles rather than boost your circulation.

Precautions

Although Pilates is a perfectly safe form of exercise for everyone, at any age, there are still some things you should consider. As with any exercise program, it is important to consult your doctor before you start if you are receiving treatment for a medical condition, have not exercised regularly for some time, if you have had a significant injury, or if you are pregnant, post-menopausal, or suffer severe menstrual symptoms.

warm-ups

introduction

The warm-up exercises on the following pages will help you release any tension held in the mind or body before you start on your Pilates session. They will also mobilize and stabilize the central core and stretch all the muscles in preparation for the more demanding exercises. It is essential to do these warm-ups, whether you will then be moving on to the Introductory, Beginner, or Advanced Level exercises.

If you are completely new to the Pilates system, you can limit your session to the warm-up exercises only, just for a week or two, while you start to put into practice the techniques and principles you learned in the previous section. The gentle actions will make you aware of the importance of developing the really strong, stable central core from which all movement stems. They will get you used to relaxing the shoulder girdle, spine, and pelvis into the neutral position, engaging the pelvic floor and abdominal muscles, and breathing laterally as you carry out the exercises, as well as inhaling and exhaling at the appropriate moment.

At first, repeat each movement only three to five times (on each side of the body, where relevant), carefully observing your body's reaction to the moves. As you become familiar with the warm-up moves, increase the number of repetitions—adding an extra one at each session—to a maximum of ten. Relax, concentrate, and work slowly and steadily, following the directions precisely. Do not try to push any of the moves too far, too soon—you are making progress the whole time, even if it does not seem that way. Always keep the principles in mind and always think "quality."

It is also a good idea to stick to the warm-up movements only for a short while if you have not taken any form of exercise for some time and perhaps feel stiff and inflexible as a result. You may find that this stage is enough of a challenge in itself at first, but in no time at all you will have loosened up your joints and started to improve your muscle tone, and you will feel ready, able and keen to tackle the next step.

The warm-up exercises are also ideal for mobilizing you first thing in the morning—after all, no self-respecting cat would wake up after a long sleep and start moving about without first having a good stretch in all directions! And they are a quick and effective way to iron out the kinks—both in the body and the mind—that tend to accumulate during a busy working day. Remember, however, that the warm-up exercises are not a "quick fix"—you must always put the full amount of focus and concentration into preparation and execution.

Most importantly, do remember—whatever stage you are at—to think positively and keep visualizing your goal as you work through each movement. There's that fit, healthy and confident new you out there, either waiting to be discovered or anxious to be maintained!

focus on breath

Aim: To focus your attention on your posture and breathing.

Benefits: The mind and the whole body.

1 STEP ONE
Stand upright with your shoulders and spine in neutral. Place your feet hip-width apart, keep your knees soft, and let your arms hang loosely by your sides.

2 STEP TWO
Close your eyes and focus on your breathing. Inhale through your nose, and visualize clean, energizing air entering your body and filling your lungs.

3 STEP THREE
Exhale, expelling all the stale air from your system. Continue breathing in this way, making sure your body stays relaxed. At first, inhale and exhale like this five times, increasing to a maximum of ten.

shrugs

Aim: To release tension from the neck and shoulders.

Benefits: Shoulders, neck, and upper body.

1 STEP ONE

Stand upright with your shoulder girdle and spine in neutral. Place your feet hip-width apart, keep your knees soft, and let your arms hang loosely by your sides. Focus on your breathing, with eyes closed if you wish.

2 STEP TWO

Inhale, and lift your shoulders up toward your ears.

3 STEP THREE

Exhale, and draw the shoulder blades into neutral. At first, do the shrugs five times, increasing to a maximum of ten.

rolling down

Aim: To mobilize the spine and and connect with the center.

Benefits: The spine, shoulders, and upper body.

1 STEP ONE
Stand upright with your shoulder girdle and spine in neutral. Place your feet hip-width apart, keep your knees soft, and let your arms hang loosely by your sides. Close your eyes and focus your attention on your breathing.

2 STEP TWO
Inhale, and lengthen through the spine.

4 STEP FOUR
Only roll down to your point of comfort—do not try to go too far too soon. At the bottom of the move, inhale, feeling the air inflate your spine and keeping the pelvic floor muscles and abdominals engaged.

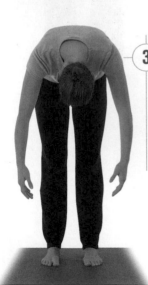

3 STEP THREE
Exhale, engaging the pelvic floor muscles and TVA, navel to spine at 30%. Gently nod your chin toward your chest, then roll forward, keeping the ribcage soft and rolling toward the hips. Sense each vertebra rolling, one at a time.

5 STEP FIVE
Roll back up, one vertebra at a time. As you finish the roll, exhale and release the shoulder blades to neutral. At first, do the roll five times, increasing to a maximum of ten.

head turns

Aim: To release tension from the neck.

Benefits: The neck and shoulders.

1 **STEP ONE**
Stand upright with your shoulder girdle and spine in neutral. Place your feet hip-width apart, keep your knees soft, and let your arms hang loosely by your sides.

2 **STEP TWO**
Inhale, to prepare.

4 **STEP FOUR**
Inhale, and return to center. Repeat the movement five times in this direction.

3 **STEP THREE**
Exhale, engaging the pelvic floor muscles and TVA, navel to spine at 30%. Turn your head to look over your right shoulder, keeping your head in line with your gaze on the horizon.

5 **STEP FIVE**
Repeat the movement five times in the opposite direction.

pivot

Aim: To mobilize the whole body and promote coordination.

Benefits: The spine, shoulders, hips, arms, and legs.

1 **STEP ONE**
Stand upright with your shoulder girdle and spine in neutral. Place your feet wider than hip-width apart, keep your knees soft, and let your arms hang loosely by your sides. Inhale, engaging the pelvic floor muscles and TVA, navel to spine at 30%. Lengthen through the spine.

2 **STEP TWO**
Exhale, and twist your body to one side. Let your arms swing loosely, moving with you. Your legs will also twist with the movement.

3 **STEP THREE**
Inhale, and twist back to the center.

4 **STEP FOUR**
Exhale, and twist to the other side.

5 **STEP FIVE**
Inhale, and twist back to the center.

6 **STEP SIX**
Each time you twist, raise your arms higher, until they reach over your head, then work them back down to your sides, in a continuous, flowing movement. Take three twists in each direction to get to the top of the movement, and three more twists in each direction to get back down.

shell stretch

Aim: To stretch and lengthen the spine.

Benefits: The spine, shoulders, neck, and abdomen.

1 **STEP ONE**
Kneel on all fours, with your knees under your hips and your arms in line with your shoulders, with the elbows soft but not locked. Drop your head between your arms.

2 **STEP TWO**
Inhale, to prepare.

3 **STEP THREE**
Exhale, engaging the pelvic floor muscles and TVA, navel to spine at 30%. Lower your bottom to your heels, keeping your hands on the floor in front of you and your head resting between your elbows. Hold this position for 15–20 seconds as you inhale and exhale, keeping the center connected. Feel the spine lengthen on the inhale.

PROGRESSION

Once you are at ease with this movement, you can increase the intensity of the stretch. Starting from Step 3, ease your buttocks off your heels and "walk" your hands a farther 6–8 inches. With both palms down flat and your head between your elbows, ease your buttocks back toward your heels. This time the stretch will also be felt in your upper back and shoulders.

4 ### STEP FOUR

Inhale, and lift your bottom off your heels. Move your hands out 4–5 inches farther, then exhale and lower your bottom back to your heels, keeping the center connected. Again, hold this position for 15–20 seconds as you inhale and exhale, keeping the center connected. Feel the stretch in the upper back and shoulders on the inhale.

5 ### STEP FIVE

Exhale, and relax.

cat stretch

Aim: To mobilize the spine and help with stabilisation.

Benefits: The spine, shoulders, neck, and abdomen.

1 **STEP ONE**
Kneel on all fours, with your spine and shoulder girdle in neutral, your knees under your hips and your hands under your shoulders. Keep your elbows slightly kinked, but not locked.

2 **STEP TWO**
Inhale, keeping your body in neutral.

3 **STEP THREE**
Exhale, engaging the pelvic floor and pulling your navel back to your spine. Keep the abdominals scooped to the spine for support. Flex the spine, curling from the tail bone toward the head.

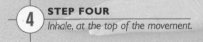

4 **STEP FOUR**
Inhale, at the top of the movement.

5 **STEP FIVE**
*Exhale, and lengthen through the spine
to the start position, keeping the spine
in neutral.*

6 **STEP SIX**
Inhale, to prepare.

7 **STEP SEVEN**
*Exhale, and repeat the movement.
Start with five repetitions and
increase to a maximum of ten.*

mermaid (side bend)

Aim: To stretch and flex the spine, with the core connected.

Benefits: The shoulders, neck, spine, and abdominals.

1 STEP ONE
Stand upright with your shoulder girdle and spine in neutral. Place your feet hip-width apart, keep your knees soft, and let your arms hang loosely by your sides.

2 STEP TWO
Standing tall and relaxed, inhale and take the left arm above your head, with the fingers pointing to the sky. Stretch through your fingers, keeping the arm strong.

3 **STEP THREE**
Exhale, and side bend to the right, keeping your pelvis in neutral. Let your head and arm follow your spine.

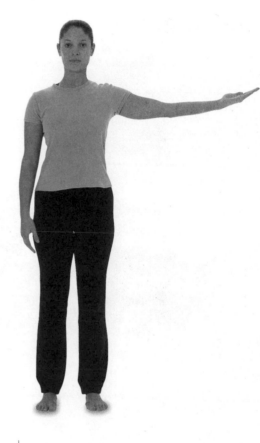

4 **STEP FOUR**
Inhale, and float back up to center, keeping your arm extended.

5 **STEP FIVE**
Exhale, and let your arm flow back down by your side. Slide your shoulder blades back into neutral, making sure there is no tension in the head, neck, and shoulder complex.

6 **STEP SIX**
Repeat the movement to the left. Do a total of five side bends on each side.

c-curve

Aim: To mobilize the spine and strengthen the central core.

Benefits: The spine, neck, shoulders, and abdominals.

STEP ONE
1
Sit on the floor, with your knees bent, your weight evenly distributed over both sitting bones and your spine in neutral.

STEP TWO
2
Place your hands lightly behind your knees. This will give you support and feedback, but do not pull on your hands as you carry out the move. Relax your shoulders, with the shoulder blades melting down your back. Inhale, and sense the inflation, elongating through the spine.

MODIFICATION

Relax your feet and lift your toes, resting only your heels on the floor. This will take the tension out of your hip flexors and so release the muscles.

3 **STEP THREE**

Exhale, engaging the pelvic floor muscles and TVA, navel to spine at 30%. Rock back off the pelvis toward the floor.

4 **STEP FOUR**

Pause, inhale and return to the upright start position. Keep the abdominals scooped and hollowed throughout the whole move for support. Only go as far as you can each time without shuddering or lifting your feet off the floor. Repeat the movement five times, increasing to a maximum of ten.

trunk rotation

Aim: To strengthen and stabilize the central core.

Benefits: The neck, abdomen, and hips.

① STEP ONE
Lie on your back, with your knees bent and your feet flat on the floor. Extend your arms out to the side of your body at shoulder level, with your palms down. Relax your spine and shoulder girdle into neutral, and let your chest soften. Engage the abdominal and pelvic floor muscles.

② STEP TWO
Inhale, wide and full.

3 STEP THREE

Exhale, and roll your knees to the right, keeping your head in neutral and both shoulders connected to the floor, with the shoulder blades in neutral. Inhale.

4 STEP FOUR

Exhale, as you return your knees to the center.

5 STEP FIVE

Repeat the movement in the opposite direction. Do the exercise a total of five times in each direction.

shoulder shrugs

Aim: To release any tension created in the shoulders during the warm-up.

Benefits: The shoulders, neck, and spine.

1 STEP ONE
Lie on your back, with your knees bent and your feet flat on the floor. Extend your arms out to the side of your body at shoulder level, with your palms down. Let your chest soften.

2 STEP TWO
Relax your spine and shoulder girdle into neutral. Engage the abdominal and pelvic floor muscles.

3 **STEP THREE**
Inhale, and lift the shoulders toward the ears.

4 **STEP FOUR**
Exhale, and draw the shoulders blades into neutral. Do the shrugs five times, increasing to a maximum of ten.

introductory
level exercises

introduction

When you arrive at the stage where you are ready to start practicing the introductory level exercises, do the warm-up exercises followed by these exercises at least twice a week for about six to eight weeks. At first, repeat each movement only three to five times (working on each side of the body, where relevant), building up to a maximum of ten times, and as always aim for slow and steady progress.

Some of the movements in this section will already be familiar to you from the warm-up section, and will reinforce the process of strengthening and stabilizing the central core. Read each exercise carefully and make sure you understand it before you start working through the steps. Take it gently, making sure you inhale and exhale at the right points, and that you keep the center connected—it's easy to let these things go while you are concentrating on the intricacies of the move itself. Remember the importance of precision!

This section introduces the Pilates leg exercises. They are very effective, and as long as you pay attention to detail, you will get fantastic results in the hip and thigh areas. Detail in this case means aligning the body correctly by keeping the pelvis in neutral and the hips stacked one above the other. It also means working the muscle in the optimum position. Do not simply swing the leg up and down or raise and lower it aimlessly—make sure you really experience the movement, feeling the muscle as it lifts and lowers your leg. Have total control over both the up phase and the down phase—it will help to imagine that you are working against some form of resistance, such as gently flowing water.

Follow these simple guidelines to help you achieve and maintain the correct alignment when you are lying on your side for the leg exercises:

• When you have one arm extended away from you and your leg or legs extended to a point at the toes, make sure you are in a straight line through the head and body from fingertip to toe, with no grip or tension in the shoulder.

• Make sure your hips are stacked one above the other, and that you are tipping neither forward nor back—place your upper hand across your navel with your fingertips on the floor to give you some support and feedback.

• Keep the top shoulder relaxed, with the shoulder blade gliding down toward your pelvis—the shoulder should not move throughout the exercise, so a glass of water could be safely placed there!

• Position the bottom leg in a figure 4 to give you a stable base (as you advance, you narrow the angle, making the base of support less stable, until eventually the angle is only very slight).

• When raising and lowering the leg, do not make huge movements—lift to an angle of about 30 degrees, and lower to hip height.

• Keep the body steady, without movement except in the working leg.

• Keep the center connected, with the pelvic floor drawn up and the navel drawn back toward the spine, and resist the temptation to let the stomach muscles contract and relax.

breathing

Aim: To strengthen the central core by activating the transversus abdominus through breathing.

Benefits: The transversus abdominus, lumbar multifidus, and pelvic floor muscles.

1 **STEP ONE**
Lie on your back, with your knees at 45 degrees, your feet flat on the floor, hip-distance apart, and your shoulder girdle in neutral. Rest your hands palms down, one on either side of your ribcage.

2 **STEP TWO**
Inhale wide and full, feeling your ribcage expand and your breath going into your back and sides.

3 STEP THREE

Exhale, gently drawing up the pelvic floor and activating the TVA in and up (MVC 30%). Feel your ribcage close in and soften, as if funneling down to the hips.

NOTE

You will be lying on your back for many of the Pilates exerices. This exercise will help you learn to stay relaxed and connected with the breath while you are in this position.

4 STEP FOUR

Continue to inhale and exhale as above, focusing your attention on your breathing. At first, inhale and exhale five times, increasing to a maximum of ten.

5 STEP FIVE

Remember your breath is gentle, not forced. Exhale through the mouth, keeping the jaw relaxed, and do not be tempted to blow through pursed lips.

neutral to imprinted spine (50/50)

Aim: the aim of this exercise is simply to help you position the spine into neutral when you are lying on your back.

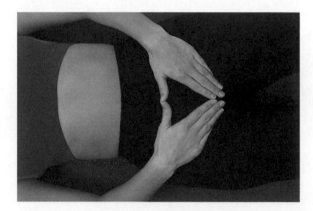

STEP ONE

1 Lie on your back, with your knees at 45 degrees and your feet flat on the floor. Place your hands on your stomach, making a triangle with your thumbs in a line at the base of your navel and your fingers splayed downwards, coming together to make a point at the pubic bone (this will provide feedback as you carry out the movement). Relax your shoulder girdle and spine into neutral.

 STEP TWO

2 Inhale wide and full, feeling your ribcage expand and your breath going into your back and sides.

 STEP THREE

3 Exhale, engaging your pelvic floor muscles and TVA. Simultaneously draw the pubic bone toward the navel and gently tilt the pelvis toward you, rolling your tail bone off the floor. You need to identify with the position of the lower abdominals at the front of the body, from the navel to the pubic bone, so imagine this movement as a "grab" from the front, rather than a push from behind.

4 **STEP FOUR**
Inhale, and release the pelvis to neutral.

5 **STEP FIVE**
Exhale, and arch the back gently.

6 **STEP SIX**
Inhale, and release the pelvis to neutral.

7 **STEP SEVEN**
Repeat the inhale and the exhale five times each at first, increasing to a maximum of ten. Check that the pelvis has come back to neutral properly each time.

lower abdominals 1

Aim: To strengthen the central core.

Benefits: The lower abdominal muscles.

STEP ONE

1 *Lie on your back, with your knees at 45 degrees and your feet flat on the floor, hip-distance apart. Either rest your arms at your sides, palms down, or lay your hands in a triangle on your stomach as in the previous exercise. Relax your shoulder girdle and spine into neutral.*

STEP TWO

2 *Inhale wide and full.*

NOTE

This is a challenging exercise as you need to maintain the core connection while breathing naturally. You also need to make sure you are activating the tilt from the muscles of the lower abdominals and not the gluteus maximus (buttocks).

3 STEP THREE

Exhale, draw up the pelvic floor muscles and draw back the navel to the spine to 30%. Simultaneously, draw the pubic bone toward the navel and, using your abdominals, gently tilt the pelvis toward you, rolling your tail bone off the floor. As in the previous exercise, this is a "grab" from the front, not a push from behind.

4 STEP FOUR

Inhale, and hold the tilt, keeping the TVA contraction activated at 30%.

5 STEP FIVE

Exhale, as you roll back to neutral.

6 STEP SIX

Repeat the exercise five times at first, increasing to a maximum of ten. Each time, hold the position for one inhale and one exhale, keeping the abdominals scooped and hollowed. As you become familiar with the movement, you can progress to two inhales and two exhales as you hold the position, and then gradually increase to a maximum of ten inhales and ten exhales.

abdominals 1

Aim: To flex the spine and strengthen the central core.

Benefits: The neck, shoulders, spine, and abdominals.

1 STEP ONE

Lie on your back, with your knees at 45 degrees and your feet in line with your knees. Rest your arms by your sides, palms down. Lengthen your neck, and relax your upper body, keeping your shoulder girdle neutral.

2 STEP TWO

Inhale and lengthen through the back of your neck by gently nodding or rocking your chin to your chest. Do not jam your chin into your chest or raise your head—just imagine your neck lengthening on the floor.

3 STEP THREE

Exhale, activate the pelvic floor and navel to spine (30%), then flex forward, letting your head and shoulders curl off the floor and bringing the ribcage toward the pelvis. Raise your arms off the floor, level with your shoulders. Make sure your pelvic floor muscles and TVA are engaged, navel to spine, and that your spine remains neutral. Do not lead with the head and shoulders—let the flexion come from the center.

4 STEP FOUR

Inhale, maintaining flexion. Make sure the pelvic floor stays drawn up and you maintain navel to spine. Resist the temptation to release the body back—keep focused forward, with the abdominals hollowing out.

5 STEP FIVE

Exhale, and lower and roll the body back to the floor. Repeat the movement five times at first, increasing to a maximum of ten.

leg slide

Aim: To stabilize the pelvis.

Benefits: The center connection and the hip flexors/extensors.

① STEP ONE

Lie on your back, with your knees bent at 45 degrees and your feet flat on the floor. Rest your arms by your sides, palms down and elbows slightly kinked. Relax your shoulder girdle and spine into neutral and engage the pelvic floor and navel to spine.

② STEP TWO

Inhale, wide and full.

3 **STEP THREE**

Exhale, drawing up and back, and slide one leg away along the floor until it is fully extended, keeping the heel in contact with the floor.

PROGRESSION

As you become familiar with this exercise and your stabilization improves, you can progress to alternating the legs. However, make sure that you are strong enough to do this without rocking the pelvis.

4 **STEP FOUR**

Inhale, keeping your leg straight.

5 **STEP FIVE**

Exhale, draw up and back, and slide the leg back up to 45 degrees.

6 **STEP SIX**

Repeat the movement five times, then change to the other leg. Increase the repetition to a maximum of ten on each leg.

knee folds

Aim: To stabilize the pelvis, strengthen the lower abdominals and mobilize at the hips.

Benefits: Transversus abdominus and hip flexors/extensors.

1 STEP ONE

Lie on your back, with your knees bent at 45 degrees and your feet flat on the floor. Rest your arms by your sides, palms down. Relax your shoulder girdle and spine into neutral and engage the pelvic floor and navel to spine.

2 STEP TWO

Inhale, wide and full.

3 STEP THREE

Exhale and let one knee float slowly up toward the ceiling, as if being pulled by an invisible string. Stop when the knee is in line with the hip and the angle of the knee is 90 degrees.

STEP FOUR
Inhale, maintaining 30% TVA activation and keeping the leg bent at 90 degrees.

STEP FIVE
Exhale, lowering your foot to the mat with the knee bent at 45 degrees. Do not let the back arch as you return the foot to the floor, and keep the center connected and strong.

PROGRESSION

As with the previous exercise, you can progress to alternating the legs once your stabilization improves. Make sure that you are strong enough to do this without rocking the pelvis. Be very careful not to let the abdominals dome and the back arch as you replace the foot to the floor.

STEP SIX
Repeat the movement five times, then change to the other leg. Increase the repetition to a maximum of ten on either leg.

flowing arms

When carrying out this exercise, it is essential that you maintain trunk organization so that the back does not arch and the ribcage does not pop off the floor. Until you have mastered the movement, only take your arm back over your head as far as it will go without your losing the rib connection.

Aim: To stabilize the shoulder girdle.

Benefits: The shoulders and abdominals.

① STEP ONE

Lie on your back, with your knees bent at 45 degrees and your feet flat on the floor. Rest your arms on the floor beside you, palms down, but make them strong, with a slight bend in the elbows. Relax your shoulder girdle into neutral.

② STEP TWO

Inhale, wide and full, and raise one arm until it is at chest level with the fingers pointing toward the sky.

3 STEP THREE

Exhale, engaging the pelvic floor muscles and TVA and keeping the spine neutral. Take the arm back as if to touch the floor (you may not be able to go all the way back at first). Keep the pelvis in neutral, the abdominals engaged with the ribcage, the ribs sliding toward the hip bones, and the shoulder blades melting down your back, with the shoulder girdle stable.

PROGRESSION

Once you are confident that you are able to keep the pelvic girdle in neutral, alternate the arms, working them both together in a flowing movement, so that one arm flows up over your head as the other flows down to the floor.

4 STEP FOUR

Inhale as you start to return the arm to the mid-position.

5 STEP FIVE

Exhale, and lower the arm to the floor. Repeat the movement five times, gradually increasing to a maximum of ten.

6 STEP SIX

Repeat the exercise with the other arm.

trunk rotation

In this exercise you rotate your head in the opposite direction to your legs, being careful to maintain the shoulder connection to the floor.

Aim: To strengthen and stabilize the central core.

Benefits: The neck, abdomen, and hips.

1 STEP ONE

Lie on your back, with your knees bent and your feet flat on the floor. Extend your arms out to the sides at shoulder level, with your palms up to let the shoulder blades remain in neutral. Relax your spine and shoulder girdle into neutral, and let your chest soften. Engage the abdominal and pelvic floor muscles.

2 STEP TWO

Inhale, wide and full.

3 STEP THREE

Exhale, and engage the pelvic floor muscles and TVA. Roll your head in one direction and your knees in the other. Exhale, and roll your knees to the right and your head to the left, keeping both shoulders connected to the floor, with the shoulder blades in neutral.

4 **STEP FOUR**
Inhale. Exhale, as you return your knees and
head to the center.

5 **STEP FIVE**
Exhale, as you return your
knees and head to the center.

6 **STEP SIX**
Repeat the movement five times to one side,
increasing to a maximum of ten, then
change to the opposite side.

c-curve

This is a progression of the warm-up exercise. This time, position your hands lightly on the sides of your knees. Try to unroll farther each time you practice the movement but only go as far as you can comfortably, without losing form.

Aim: To mobilize the spine and strengthen the central core.

Benefits: The spine, neck, shoulders, and abdominals.

1 **STEP ONE**

Sit on the floor, with your weight evenly distributed over both sitting bones and your spine in neutral. Relax your shoulders, with the shoulder blades melting down your back.

2 **STEP TWO**

Inhale, and sense the inflation, elongating through the spine.

3 **STEP THREE**

With the points of your toes gently touching the floor, engage the pelvic floor muscles and TVA navel to spine at 30%. Connect with the center, slowly roll backwards off the pelvis. Rock slightly back and forth.

4 **STEP FOUR**

Balancing on your toes, inhale as you roll back to the start position. Repeat the movement five times, gradually increasing to a maximum of ten.

MODIFICATION

Relax your feet and lift your toes, resting only your heels on the floor (this will take the tension out of your hip flexors).

spine stretch

Aim: To lengthen the muscles of the spine.

Benefits: The neck, shoulders, spine, hips, and abdominals.

1 ### STEP ONE
Sit on the floor, with your weight evenly distributed over both sitting bones, and your legs extended hip-width apart (if the hamstrings are too tight, bend your knees slightly or sit on a rolled-up towel or mat). Lengthen your spine, so that the crown of the head is reaching toward the ceiling.

2 ### STEP TWO
Extend your arms in front of you, slightly below shoulder level, palms facing up. Relax the shoulder girdle into neutral.

3 ### STEP THREE
Inhale, and lengthen the spine, lifting up from the hips.

4 ### STEP FOUR
Exhale, engaging the pelvic floor and TVA. Curl the chin to the chest, but do not force it. Keep the abdominals scooped so that the ribs float to the hips. Curl out toward your feet as if rolling over a large beach ball.

5 STEP FIVE

Inhale as you slowly unfurl, one vertebra at a time, until the spinal column is restacked.

6 STEP SIX

Exhale, bringing up your head and letting your shoulder blades slide back down. Repeat the movement five times, increasing gradually to a maximum of ten.

spine twist

Aim: To strengthen and mobilize the spine.

Benefits: The obliques, lumbar multifidus, transversus abdominus, and shoulder girdle.

1 STEP ONE

Sit on the floor, with your weight evenly distributed over both sitting bones. Extend your legs, with your inner thighs touching, or sit in the cross-legged "tailor" position. Lengthen your spine so that the crown of your head reaches toward the ceiling. Cross your arms over your chest, and relax the shoulder girdle into neutral.

2 STEP TWO

Inhale.

PROGRESSION

When you are confident about your position and control, alternate the twist to one side, then the other, increasing from five repetitions each side to a maximum of ten.

3 **STEP THREE**

Exhale, engaging the pelvic floor muscles and TVA. Lift out of your hips and slowly turn to one side, using the waist.

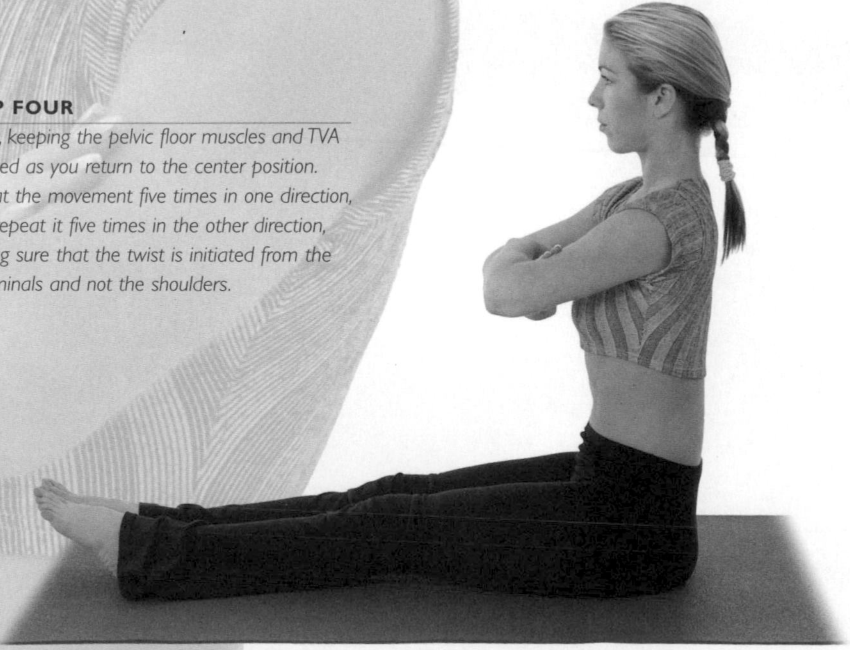

4 **STEP FOUR**

Inhale, keeping the pelvic floor muscles and TVA engaged as you return to the center position. Repeat the movement five times in one direction, then repeat it five times in the other direction, making sure that the twist is initiated from the abdominals and not the shoulders.

swan dive 1

Aim: To strengthen and stabilize the shoulder girdle and spine, and work the spine extensors.

Benefits: The shoulders, spine, transversus abdominus, hamstring, and gluteus maximus.

1 **STEP ONE**
Lie face down, with your forehead resting on the floor on a folded towel or soft pillow. Rest your arms by your sides, palms down, and relax your shoulders into neutral. Keep your inner thighs connected and your feet pointed.

2 **STEP TWO**
Inhale, lengthening through your spine and sliding your shoulder blades down your back.

3 **STEP THREE**
Exhale, engaging the pelvic floor muscles and TVA.

(4) STEP FOUR

Inhale, peeling your upper body off the floor from the hips. Lengthen through the back, pulling your shoulder blades down. Keep the abdominals engaged for support. Keep the chest wide open and the shoulders in neutral. Keep your eyes focused on the floor and do not push back the neck and head.

(5) STEP FIVE

Exhale, and lower your upper body to the floor, drawing in the navel and pelvic floor. Repeat the movement five times, increasing to a maximum of ten.

swimming

Aim: To lengthen the spine and legs.

Benefits: Shoulders, spine extensors, and transversus abdominus.

3 STEP THREE
Exhale, and lift your left leg off the floor. Point the toes and lengthen the leg away from the body, keeping the neck long and the pelvis and ribs in alignment.

1 **STEP ONE**
Lie face down, with your forehead resting on
your hands and your legs extended. Relax
the spine and shoulder girdle into neutral.

2 **STEP TWO**
Inhale, engaging the pelvic floor
muscles and TVA.

4 **STEP FOUR**
Inhale as you return to the start position.

5 **STEP FIVE**
Repeat the movement with the right leg.
Repeat the whole exercise five times,
increasing to a maximum of ten.

forward leg kick

The following exercises are carried out as a series, so work through them both on one leg first, then repeat them on the other leg. Repeat each movement five times at first, gradually increasing to a maximum of ten.

Aim: To strengthen the lower back, mobilize the hips, and work the buttocks and hamstrings.

Benefits: The hip flexors, transversus abdominus, and gluteus maximus.

1 **STEP ONE**

Lie on your side with your lower arm fully extended, palm up. With the hips stacked one on top of the other, bend the lower leg into a figure 4. The top leg should be straight and hovering at hip height. Keep your top shoulder relaxed and drape your free hand and arm over your navel. Relax the shoulder girdle into neutral.

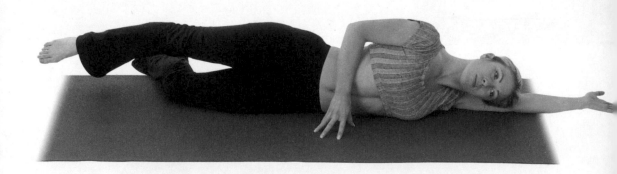

2 STEP TWO

Inhale, and engage the pelvic floor muscles and TVA. Dorsiflex the upper foot, stretching through the heel, and draw the leg forward to 90 degrees. Maintain a neutral pelvis.

3 STEP THREE

Exhale, plantarflex the foot and draw back the leg to its starting position, keeping the leg at hip height and maintaining a neutral pelvis.

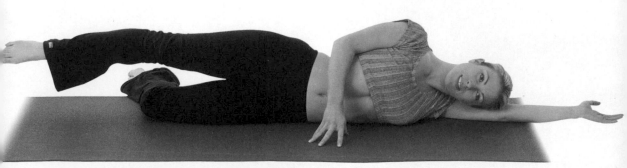

top leg lift

Aim: To mobilize the hips and work the buttocks and hamstrings.

Benefits: The hip flexors, transversus abdominus, gluteus maximus, and hamstrings.

1 STEP ONE

Lie on your side with your lower arm fully extended, palm up. With the hips stacked one on top of the other, bend the lower leg into a figure 4. The top leg should be straight and hovering at hip height. Keep your top shoulder relaxed and drape your free hand and arm over your navel. Relax the shoulder girdle into neutral.

2 **STEP TWO**

Inhale and engage the pelvic floor muscles and TVA. Plantarflex the foot and lift the leg slightly.

3 **STEP THREE**

Exhale, and lower the leg to its starting position.

beginner level
exercises

introduction

By now, you will be very familiar with the unique language of Pilates—core stability, neutral position, lateral breathing, and so forth—so you are ready to move a step further. This section contains a large number of movements from the earlier Introductory Level Exercises, but you will find that there are now subtle changes that make them a little more challenging.

Each exercise has a panel explaining the purpose of the exercise, and of the progression where relevant. For some of the exercises, you will also find tips to help you support the movement until you are ready to carry it out unaided—for example, the Abdominals 2 exercise on pages 102 and 103 suggests a way of lightly supporting your head until your abdominals are strong enough to take over all the work. As always, you are not looking for instant results, so do not feel you are failing if you have to call on this extra support at first—just keep making slow and steady progress, and eventually you will find that you no longer need it.

Several of the exercises in this section also have suggestions for progressions and modifications to the basic movement. Move on to the progressions when you feel confident that you can carry out the basic move easily, or try sticking to a modification for a short while if the basic move is a little too challenging at first. Again, you are not failing if you do this—you are simply approaching the technique in the way Pilates intended and achieving quality, not quantity.

This section contains the original and best-known Pilates exercise—the One Hundred, so-called because you aim to inhale to the count of five and exhale to the count of five (making ten), then repeat the movement ten times (making the hundred). This exercise requires a very strong, stable center, along with controlled but rhythmic breathing, but the abdominal exercises will have prepared you for it.

The section ends with leg circles, a fantastic movement to finish off the leg exercises, working the hips, buttocks, and thighs and promoting mobility at the hip. To do these, the body must be very stable, and you must remember that the movement comes from the hip—do not be tempted just to wiggle your foot or toes from the ankle. What you are after is a small, very controlled movement, not huge circles—imagine your leg is inside a small jar, and you are working around the circumference. When you can perform this movement smoothly, keeping the shoulders in neutral and not letting the body tip either forward or back, you will know that you are well on the way to core stability.

As before, the goal of all the exercises is to start with five repetitions and build up slowly, adding one repetition at a time, until you can achieve ten repetitions in good form—that is, in a slow, controlled, flowing movement. Relax, find your rhythm, take your time, and remember that focus, precision, and breathing are still all-important.

breathing

As with the introductory level, start with this exercise to focus your attention on your breathing.

Aim: To strengthen the central core by activating the transversus abdominus through breathing.

Benefits: The transversus abdominus, lumbar multifidus, and pelvic floor muscles.

1 STEP ONE
Lie on your back, with your knees at 45 degrees, your feet flat on the floor, hip-width apart, and your shoulder girdle in neutral. Rest your hands across your ribcage.

2 STEP TWO
Inhale wide and full, feeling your ribcage expand and the breath going into your back and sides.

3 **STEP THREE**

Exhale, gently drawing up the pelvic floor and activating the TVA in and up (MVC 30%). Feel your ribcage close in and soften, as if funneling down to the hips.

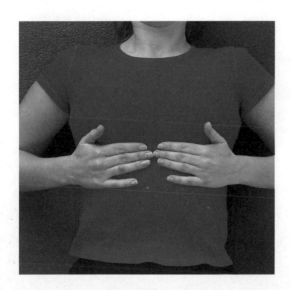

4 **STEP FOUR**

Continue to inhale and exhale as above, focusing your attention on your breathing. At first, inhale and exhale five times, increasing to a maximum of ten. Remember your breath is gentle, not forced. Exhale through the mouth, keeping the jaw relaxed, and do not be tempted to blow through pursed lips.

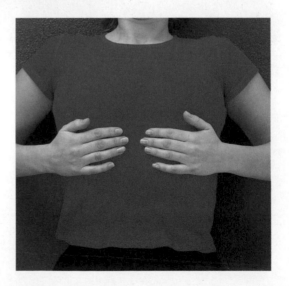

lumbar rolls

Aim: To strengthen the central core.

Benefits: The abdominal muscles.

STEP ONE

1

Lie on your back, with your knees at 45 degrees and your feet flat on the floor, hip-width apart. Place your hands on your stomach, making a triangle with your thumbs in a line at the base of your navel and your fingers splayed downward, coming together to make a point at the pubic bone (this will provide feedback as you carry out the movement). Relax your shoulder girdle and spine into neutral.

STEP TWO

2

Inhale wide and full, feeling your ribcage expand and the breath going into your back and sides.

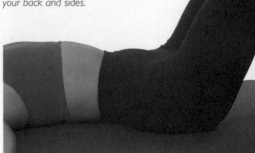

3 STEP THREE

Exhale, engaging your pelvic floor muscles and TVA. Simultaneously draw the pubic bone towards the navel and gently tilt the pelvis towards you, rolling your tail bone off the floor.

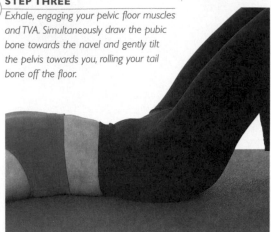

4 STEP FOUR

Inhale, and release the pelvis to neutral.

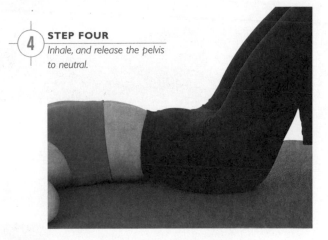

5 STEP FIVE

Exhale, and arch the back gently.

6 STEP SIX

Inhale, and release the pelvis to neutral. Repeat the movement five times, increasing gradually to a maximum of ten.

lower abdominals 2

In the introductory exercise for lower abdominals, you held the tilt as you inhaled. Now that you are familiar with the technique, hold the contraction—NOT YOUR BREATH—for 10–20 seconds, as you inhale and exhale rhythmically.

Aim: To strengthen the central core.

Benefits: The lower abdominal muscles.

STEP ONE

1 Lie on your back, with your knees at 45 degrees and your feet flat on the floor, hip-width apart. Either rest your arms at your sides, palms down, or lay your hands in a triangle on your stomach as in the previous exercise. Relax your shoulder girdle and spine into neutral.

STEP TWO

2 Inhale, wide and full.

3 STEP THREE

Exhale. Simultaneously draw the pubic bone toward the navel and, using your abdominals to initiate the movement, gently tilt the pelvis toward you.

4 STEP FOUR

Inhale, and hold the tilt, keeping the TVA contraction activated at 30% as you breathe rhythmically for 10–20 seconds.

5 STEP FIVE

Exhale, as you roll back to neutral. Repeat the movement five times, gradually increasing to a maximum of ten.

abdominals 2

In the introductory exercises for the abdominals, you held the flexion as you inhaled. In this exercise, you release the flexion by 5% as you inhale, and come back to it as you exhale, without touching the floor. Keep your gaze on your knees as you carry out the movement to ensure good head and neck placement. If you feel your head getting heavy, support it lightly with one hand, your elbow open wide like a wing—but do not clamp your head too hard and draw it forward.

Aim: To flex the spine while strengthening and stabilizing the central core.

Benefits: The neck, shoulders, spine, and abdominals.

STEP ONE

Lie on your back, with your knees at 45 degrees and your feet in line with your knees, hip-width apart. Rest your arms by your sides, palms down. Lengthen your neck, and relax your upper body, keeping your shoulder girdle neutral.

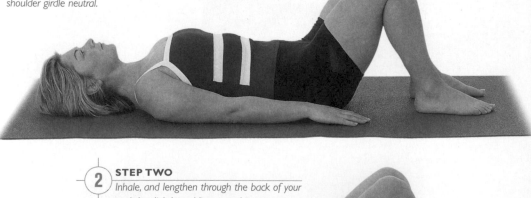

STEP TWO

Inhale, and lengthen through the back of your neck by slightly nodding your chin to your chest, without raising your head.

3 STEP THREE

Exhale, and flex forward, letting your head and shoulders curl off the floor and bringing the ribcage toward the pelvis. Raise your arms off the floor, level with your shoulders. Make sure your pelvic floor muscles and TVA are engaged, navel to spine, and that your spine remains neutral.

4 STEP FOUR

Inhale, and from the flexion release your body back by about 5% so that you extend the spine slightly while still maintaining the abdominal hollow. Do NOT return to the floor.

5 STEP FIVE

Exhale, drawing up the pelvic floor and contracting the navel to spine by 5% so that you are scooped as in Step 3. Repeat the movement five times, increasing to a maximum of ten.

one hundred

This is perhaps the most well-known of the Pilates movements, combining the main aims of Pilates—to strengthen and stabilize the central core while promoting controlled and rhythmic breathing. Mastering the Abdominals 1 and 2 movements will prepare you well for this exercise. In its most advanced form, the One Hundred includes gentle beats with the arms, but for stability the arms are kept strong but static here.

Aim: To flex the spine, stabilize the shoulder girdle and pelvis, strengthen the central core, and promote breath control.

Benefits: The neck, shoulders, spine, abdominals, and breathing.

1 STEP ONE
Lie on your back, with your knees at 45 degrees, your feet flat on the floor and your inner thighs connected. Rest your arms by your sides, palms down, but keep them strong, with a slight bend in the elbows. Relax the shoulder girdle into neutral.

2 STEP TWO
Inhale, and lengthen through the back of the neck.

3 STEP THREE

Exhale, and flex forward, letting your head and shoulders curl off the floor and bringing the ribcage toward the pelvis. Raise your arms off the floor and keep them strong, level with your shoulders. Make sure your pelvic floor muscles and TVA are engaged, navel to spine, and that your spine remains neutral.

4 STEP FOUR

Inhale, and count to five, maintaining the TVA contraction at 20–30%.

5 STEP FIVE

Exhale, and count to five, holding the flexion and pulling the contraction to 30%.

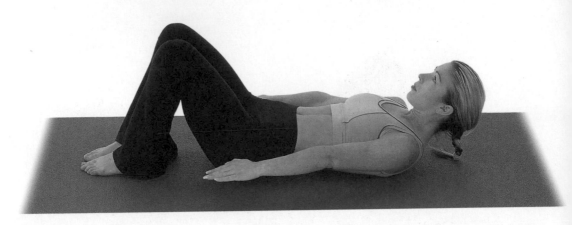

6 STEP SIX

Repeat the movement five times, gradually increasing to a maximum of ten. With each repetition, try to maintain the center connection and not let the major abdominal muscle dome.

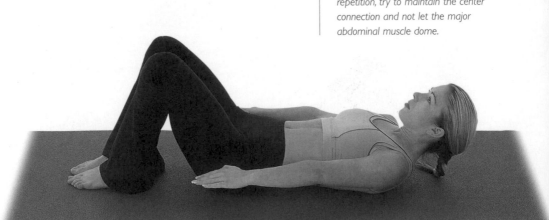

PROGRESSION

Only try these variations once you are confident of your stability, as you MUST be able to keep your pelvis and spine in neutral, without arching or straining the lower back or lifting the hips.

1 Raise one foot so that the knee is at 90 degrees, directly over the hip. To do this, inhale and roll your pelvis as in Lower Abdominals 2 (page 100), then exhale and raise one leg as in Knee Folds (page 72).

2 Raise both feet so that both knees are at 90 degrees, directly over the hip. To do this, first raise one leg as above, then inhale, maintaining the position, and exhale as you raise the other leg.

bent knee circle

This is a fantastic exercise for mobilizing the hip joints, and is particularly useful if you spend a lot of time sitting down or driving so that the muscles of the hip and inner thighs get very little stretch. When circling the knees, make sure you exhale when the leg is moving away from you, as this is when you most need stability and a good connection with the center. In its most advanced form, this movement is carried out with the leg fully extended.

Aim: To mobilize the hip joint and stretch the muscles of the hip and inner thigh.

Benefits: The abdomen, hips and inner thighs.

1 **STEP ONE**
Lie on your back, with your knees bent at 45 degrees and your feet flat on the floor, hip-width apart. Rest your arms by your sides, palms down, or place them on your stomach in a triangle for feedback—the sides of the triangle should remain even as you carry out the movement. Relax your shoulder girdle and spine into neutral.

2 **STEP TWO**
Inhale.

3 **STEP THREE**
Exhale, engaging the pelvic floor muscles and TVA, and take one knee up to 90 degrees, in line with the hip. Hold the position.

4 STEP FOUR

Inhale, keeping the pelvic floor muscles and TVA engaged. Circle the knee clockwise toward you to the mid line, keeping the leg stationary—imagine you are stirring the leg in the hip socket.

5 STEP FIVE

Exhale, completing the circle by taking the knee away from you.

6 STEP SIX

Continue, circling the knee five times clockwise and five times counterclockwise.

7 STEP SEVEN

Repeat the movement with the other leg.

PROGRESSION

Take both knees to 90 degrees, and place your fingers on your kneecaps. This time, create only small circles, using your fingers to give you feedback that your legs are moving evenly. When circling both legs like this, it is essential to keep the pelvis stable so that the back does not arch off the floor.

rolling

Aim: Abdominal connection and spinal articulation stretch of the erector spine muscles.

Benefits: The spine, neck, shoulders, and abdominals.

1 STEP ONE

Sit on the floor, sitting up on the sit bones, with the spine flexed forward as in the C Curve, and with the pelvis slightly tilted away, i.e., tucked under. Your knees should be bent at 45 degrees and your legs connected. Place your hands on your shins and keep your shoulders in neutral.

2 STEP TWO

Inhale. Follow your pelvic tilt and C Curve by rolling back to the floor behind you.

3 **STEP THREE**
Exhale. Keep your gaze on your knees and your head in the slightly forward, C Curve position.

4 **STEP FOUR**
Keeping the center connected and the legs in line with the hands, roll back to the start, staying balanced.

single leg stretch

This exercise is a more challenging progression of the sliding leg movement. Start slowly, keeping the body flat and the legs at 90 degrees. Stretch your legs out at a pace that lets you keep your body in neutral. As you gain strength and control over the central core, flex the body before stretching out the legs.

Aim: To promote coordination, to strengthen and stabilize the abdominals, and to stretch the leg muscles.

Benefits: The neck, shoulders, transversus abdominus, hip flexors (eccentrically), and hip extensors and quadriceps (concentrically).

① STEP ONE
Lie on your back, with your inner thighs connected, your knees bent at 45 degrees and your feet flat on the floor. Rest your arms by your sides with your palms down and a slight bend in your elbows.

② STEP TWO
Inhale, lengthening through the back of the neck.

3 **STEP THREE**

Exhale, and initiate the pelvic tilt, engaging the pelvic floor muscles and the TVA, navel to spine, and keeping the spine neutral. Keeping the inner thighs connected, raise both knees to 90 degrees.

4 **STEP FOUR**

Inhale, maintaining the position.

5 **STEP FIVE**

Exhale and flex forward, letting the head and shoulders curl off the floor and bringing the ribcage toward the pelvis. Raise your arms to shoulder level. Keep the pelvic floor muscles and TVA engaged, navel to spine, and neutral spine.

6 **STEP SIX**

Inhale, to prepare.

7 STEP SEVEN
Exhale, stretching one leg away from the body but maintaining the TVA contraction.

8 STEP EIGHT
Inhale, returning the leg to center.

MODIFICATIONS

If you are unable to perform this exercise, substitute the leg slides from the Introductory level, then carry on with the remainder of the exercises from this level.

STEP NINE

9

Exhale, stretching the other leg away from the body. Repeat the exercise five times in a cycling movement, gradually increasing to a maximum of ten.

double leg stretch

This movement requires a very strong and stable central core, especially as you progress. You can raise one leg at a time or both together, depending on your level of stability.

Aim: To promote coordination, to strengthen and stabilize the abdominals, and to stretch the leg muscles.

Benefits: The transversus abdominus, pectorals, and hip flexors (eccentrically and concentrically)

1 **STEP ONE**

Lie on your back, with your inner thighs connected, your knees bent at 45 degrees and your feet flat on the floor, hip-width apart. Rest your arms by your sides with your palms down and a slight bend in your elbows.

2 **STEP TWO**

Inhale, and lengthen through the cervical spine.

3 ### STEP THREE
Exhale, and initiate a pelvic tilt, engaging the pelvic floor muscles and the TVA, navel to spine, and keeping the spine neutral. Keeping the inner thighs connected, raise both knees to 90 degrees.

4 ### STEP FOUR
Inhale, maintaining the position.

5 ### STEP FIVE
Exhale, and flex forward, letting the head and shoulders curl off the floor and bringing the ribcage toward the pelvis. Raise your arms to shoulder level. Keep the pelvic floor muscles and TVA engaged, navel to spine, and neutral spine.

6 ### STEP SIX
Inhale, to prepare.

7 **STEP SEVEN**

Exhale, extending both arms and both legs away from the center line.

8 **STEP EIGHT**

Inhale, and return to the center. This exercise is very difficult and challenging, so aim for very slow and steady progress. Start with only three repetitions, then build up to five, then seven to eight, and eventually to ten.

MODIFICATIONS

When carrying out the modifications, flex the upper body off the floor and make sure you have a very strong, connected center. Inhale and circle your arms to the ceiling, then exhale as you draw the shoulder blades down your back, completing the circle.

The arms must be strong like a beating wing, but not tense. Your shoulders and the shoulder girdle must be stable, with the blades being drawn down as you lower the arms. This will enable you to circle (circumduct) your arms in the optimum position, without causing tension in the neck or shoulder area.

1 Flex the upper body and circle the arms from the shoulders. Keep the arms firm from shoulder to finger. Keep the knees bent at 90 degrees, or leave one at 45 degrees and bend the other to 90 degrees.

2 In Step 7, only extend the arm and leg on one side at a time.

shoulder bridge

This is an ideal exercise for rolling away the stresses of the day. It is not a pelvic thrust—the aim is to roll through the spine, segment by segment. Roll only as far as you are comfortable each time, starting with the lower abdomen, then progressing to the navel, the ribcage, and eventually to the base of the shoulder blades. At the top of the position the shoulder blades must be relaxed.

Aim: To lengthen the body and articulate through the spine.

Benefits: The transversus abdominus, the gluteus maximum, and the hamstrings.

1 STEP ONE
Lie on your back, with your knees at 45 degrees and your feet hip-width apart. Rest your arms by your sides, palms down. Lengthen your neck, and relax your upper body, keeping your shoulder girdle neutral.

2 STEP TWO
Inhale.

3 STEP THREE

Exhale, and initiate the pelvic tilt toward the ribcage, engaging the pelvic floor muscles, TVA, and navel to spine and keeping the spine in neutral. Articulate through the spine from the tail bone, one vertebra at a time, as far as the base of the shoulder blades, so that your body forms a bridge shape. Do not roll as far as the neck (cervical spine).

4 STEP FOUR

Inhale, maintaining the TVA contraction.

5 STEP FIVE

Exhale and articulate, one vertebra at a time, back to the start position, dropping the heart first, rolling into the navel, and lastly dropping the tail bone. Repeat the movement five times, gradually increasing to a maximum of ten.

spine stretch

This movement is the same as in the introductory level. However, it is essential to do this exercise at this stage, as the body needs to flex forward to balance the muscle work.

Aim: To strengthen the abdominals and lengthen the muscles of the spine.

Benefits: The abdominals, spine, and hips.

1 **STEP ONE**

Sit on the floor, with your weight evenly distributed over both sitting bones and your spine in neutral. Lengthen your spine so that the top of your head reaches toward the ceiling. Extend your legs, hip-width apart (if your hamstrings feel too tight in this position, bend your knees slightly or sit on a rolled towel or mat). Extend your arms in front of you, slightly below shoulder level, with the palms facing up to help the shoulders stay relaxed and stable. Relax the shoulder girdle into neutral.

2 **STEP TWO**

Inhale, and lift up out of the hips, elongating the spine.

3 STEP THREE

Exhale, engaging the pelvic floor muscles and TVA. Curl the chin to the chest, but do not jam it. Let the ribs float down to the hips, keeping the abdominals scooped. Curl out toward your feet as if rolling over a large beach ball.

4 STEP FOUR

Inhale as you slowly unfurl, one vertebra at a time, until the spinal column is restacked.

5 STEP FIVE

Exhale, bringing your head up last as your shoulder blades slide down your back. Repeat the movement five times, gradually increasing to a maximum of ten.

spine twist

This is another lovely, relaxing exercise. Imagine yourself as a corkscrew, exhaling as you draw up and twist, and inhaling as you unwind back to the center, maintaining the connection. At first, work one side at a time, keeping the pace even and making sure the sitting bones are even and remain on the floor. As you progress, you can work from one side to the other in a flowing movement. A further progression is to hold the twist on the exhale, then push round a little farther before inhaling and returning to the center in one movement.

Aim: To work the muscles at the waistline (obliques) and the spine rotators.

Benefits: The obliques, lumbar multifidus, transversus abdominus, and shoulder girdle.

1 STEP ONE

Sit on the floor, with your weight evenly distributed over both sitting bones and your spine in neutral. Lengthen your spine so that the top of your head reaches toward the ceiling . Extend your legs, keeping the inner thighs connected (if your hamstrings feel too tight in this position, bend your knees slightly or sit on a rolled towel or mat). Extend the arms laterally, palms up. Relax the shoulder girdle into neutral.

2 STEP TWO

Inhale.

3 **STEP THREE**

Exhale, engaging the pelvic floor muscles and TVA. Lift out of your hips and slowly turn to one side, using the abdominal contraction to initiate the movement as if drawing the navel in lateral rotation.

4 **STEP FOUR**

Inhale, maintaining the pelvic floor and TVA contraction as you return to the center position. Again, initiate the movement from the center as if drawing the navel toward the mid-line.

5 **STEP FIVE**

Repeat the movement five times one way, then repeat five times the other way. Gradually increase the repetitions to a maximum of ten. When you are confident that the pelvis is stable, alternate the twists.

swan dive 2

Positioning your hands at shoulder level in the progression exercise will help stabilize you and enable you to peel your upper body farther off the floor, but maintain control in the center and resist the temptation to push up on your hands. The shoulders must stay in neutral and the ribs and pelvis must remain integrated to ensure that the ribs do not move forward, taking the abdominals with them.

Aim: To strengthen and stabilize the shoulder girdle and spine.

Benefits: The shoulders, spine, transversus abdominus, hamstring, and gluteus maximus.

1 STEP ONE

Lie face down, with your forehead resting on the floor on a folded towel or soft pillow. Rest your arms by your sides, palms facing out, and relax your shoulders into neutral. Keep your inner thighs connected and your feet pointed.

2 STEP TWO

Inhale.

3 STEP THREE

Exhale, engaging the pelvic floor muscles and TVA and lengthening through the spine.

PROGRESSION

1. When you have achieved good form working the upper body, extend both arms together, with the shoulder blades relaxed and in neutral.
2. Combine the arm and leg movements, lifting and extending the right arm and leg together, followed by the left arm and leg.
3. Combine the arm and leg movements, lifting and extending the right arm and left leg together, followed by the left arm and right leg.

4 **STEP FOUR**

Inhale, peeling your upper body off the floor from the hips. Lengthen through the back, pulling your shoulder blades down. Keep the abdominals engaged for support. Keep the chest wide open and the shoulders in neutral. Keep your eyes focused on the floor and do not push back the neck and head.

5 **STEP FIVE**

Exhale, maintaining the connection with the center, and lower the body to the floor. Repeat the movement five times, gradually increasing to a maximum of ten.

swimming

If you have a back or hip problem, seek advice before attempting this exercise as bilateral movement can exacerbate some conditions. Take the exercise slowly, as it requires good central stability while the arms and legs are pulling away from each other. The progression exercises will promote coordination and movement integration. Your eventual aim is to extend the arms and legs from the center and beat them up and down in a swimming motion as you inhale and exhale rhythmically.

Aim: To lengthen the spine and strengthen and stabilize the center.

Benefits: The transversus abdominus, shoulder stabilizers, and spine extensors.

1 STEP ONE

Lie face down, with your forehead resting on your hands, and your legs relaxed, hip-width apart. Relax the spine and shoulder girdle into neutral.

2 STEP TWO

Inhale, engaging the pelvic floor muscles and TVA.

3 STEP THREE

Exhale, and lift your right leg off the floor. Point the toes and lengthen the leg away from the body, keeping the neck long and the pelvis and ribs in alignment.

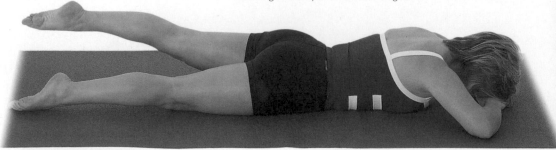

4 STEP FOUR

Inhale as you return to the start position.

5 STEP FIVE

Repeat the movement five times with the left leg, then five times with the right leg. Gradually increase the repetitions to ten. When you feel confident that your legs and pelvis are stable, alternate the legs for a total of six to ten repetitions (that is, raising each leg three to five times).

6 STEP SIX (ARMS ONLY)

Inhale, engaging the pelvic floor muscles and TVA.

7 STEP SEVEN

Exhale, and extend the right arm in front of you, off the floor. Keep your head in line with your arm, your shoulder blades melting down your back and your neck long—focus your gaze on the floor. There should be no tension in the upper body—as you extend one arm, keep the other arm folded as shown to aid stability.

8 STEP EIGHT

Inhale as you return to the start position. Repeat the movement five times with the right arm, then five times with the left arm. Gradually increase the repetitions to ten. When you feel confident that your arms and shoulders are stable, alternate the arms for a total of six to ten repetitions (that is, raising each arm three to five times).

PROGRESSION

1 When you have achieved good form with both the legs and the arms, combine the two movements, lifting the right arm and leg together, followed by the left arm and leg,
2 Combine the two movements, lifting the right arm and left leg, followed by the left arm and right leg.

cat stretch

Maintain the connection to the center throughout this exercise.
When you return the spine to the start position, do not let it
drop or sag toward the floor—imagine yourself supporting a
tray on a flat back, with the shoulders set, the head and neck in
line with the spine, and the pelvis in neutral.

Aim: To mobilize the spine and help with stabilization.

Benefits: The spine, shoulders, neck, and abdomen.

1 **STEP ONE**
*Kneel on all fours, with your spine and shoulder
girdle in neutral, your knees under your hips, and
your hands under your shoulders.*

2 **STEP TWO**
*Inhale and, keeping the body in neutral,
engage the pelvic floor muscles and TVA.*

3 **STEP THREE**

Exhale and, keeping the abdominals scooped to the spine for support, flex the spine, curling from the tail bone toward the head and dropping your head between your arms.

4 **STEP FOUR**

Inhale at the top of the movement and extend the spine so your back is arched like a cat stretching. Maintain the TVA contraction.

5 **STEP FIVE**

Exhale and uncurl the spine from the tail bone, letting the head come back up to the start position.

6 **STEP SIX**

Repeat the movement five times, gradually increasing to a maximum of ten.

superman

As with the previous exercise, maintain the connection to the center throughout this exercise, keeping the shoulders set, the head and neck in line with the spine, and the pelvis in neutral. It is a great challenge, as you extend the leg away, to keep the pelvis level and not drop the hip of the extended leg. If you have a problem with your knees and find this exercise uncomfortable, stop practicing it.

Aim: To strengthen the center and stretch and lengthen the spine and legs.

Benefits: The transversus abdominus, gluteus maximus, and hamstrings.

1 STEP ONE

Kneel on all fours, with your spine and shoulder girdle in neutral, your knees under your hips, and your hands under your shoulders.

2 STEP TWO

Inhale, engaging the pelvic floor muscles and TVA. Lengthen away from the center through the spine, tail bone, and crown.

3 STEP THREE

Exhale, maintaining the abdominal contraction. Extend the right arm away from the center, in line with the shoulder and the head. Keep the shoulder girdle organized.

4 STEP FOUR

Inhale, and return to the start position.

PROGRESSION

1 When you have achieved good form with both the legs and the arms, combine the two movements, extending the right arm and leg together, followed by the left arm and leg,

2 Combine the two movements, extending the right arm and left leg, followed by the left arm and right leg.

5 STEP FIVE

Repeat the movement five times with the right arm, then five times with the left arm. Gradually increase the repetitions to ten. When you feel confident that your arms and shoulders are stable, alternate the arms for a total of six to ten repetitions (that is, extending each arm three to five times).

6 STEP SIX

Inhale, engaging the pelvic floor muscles and TVA. Lengthen away from the center through the spine, tail bone and crown.

7 STEP SEVEN

Exhale, maintaining the abdominal contraction. Extend the right leg away from the center, in line with the hip. Keep the pelvic girdle organized.

8 STEP EIGHT

Inhale, and return to the start position.

9 STEP NINE

Repeat the movement five times with the right leg, then five times with the left leg. Gradually increase the repetitions to ten. When you feel confident that your legs are stable, alternate the legs for a total of six to ten repetitions (that is, extending each leg three to five times).

forward leg kick

For this exercise, the center needs to be really strong as the base of support is limited and the body will be inclined either to roll forward or rock back. So, although it is a leg exercise, keep thinking "center." You may find it helpful to place a small towel between your arm and your head for support—this will help to keep your neck in alignment with the spine.

Aim: To strengthen and stabilize the center and work the hips and abdomen.

Benefits: The hips, flexors, transversus abdominus, and gluteus maximus.

1 STEP ONE

Lie on your side, with your hips stacked one on top of the other and your legs together with the inner thigh connected. Extend your lower arm, palm up, so that you are in a straight line from your fingertips to your toes.

2 STEP TWO

Now angle your legs forward slightly, without changing the position of your spine, which must still be in a straight line from your head to your tail.

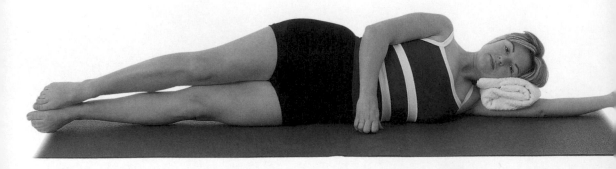

3 STEP THREE

From this position, separate the top leg and bring it back in line with your hip joint, hovering at hip height, with the foot dorsiflexed (bent). Keep the knee facing forward in the same direction as the hip—do not let it rotate toward the floor. Bend the upper arm at the elbow with the palm over your stomach, for feedback. Keep the top shoulder relaxed and in alignment, and the shoulder girdle in neutral. Rest your head on your arm to keep in line with the spine.

4 STEP FOUR

Inhale, engaging the pelvic floor muscles and TVA. With the foot dorsiflexed, stretch through the heel. Draw the leg forward to 90 degrees, maintaining a neutral pelvis—you may not be able to achieve the 90 degrees at first, so go as far as you can without losing form and progress gradually.

5 STEP FIVE

Exhale, plantarflex (stretch) the foot and draw the leg back to the start position, maintaining a neutral pelvis and keeping the leg at hip height. Repeat the movement five times with one leg, then turn over and work the other leg. Gradually increase the repetitions to a maximum of ten.

top leg lift

As with the previous exercise, the center needs to be really strong as the base of support is limited and the body will be inclined either to roll forward or rock back. So, although it is a leg exercise, keep thinking "center."

Aim: To strengthen and stabilize the center, and work the hips, abdomen, hamstrings, and calves.

Benefits: Abductors of the buttocks and top leg, and transversus abdominus.

1 STEP ONE

Lie on your side, with your hips stacked one on top of the other and your legs together with the inner thigh connected. Extend your lower arm, palm up, so that you are in a straight line from your fingertips to your toes.

2 STEP TWO

Now angle your legs forward slightly, without changing the position of your spine, which must still be in a straight line from your head to your tail.

3 STEP THREE

From this position, separate the top leg and bring it back in line with your hip joint, hovering at hip height. Point your toes. Keep the knee facing forward in the same direction as the hip—do not let it rotate toward the floor. Bend the upper arm at the elbow with the palm over your stomach, for feedback. Keep the top shoulder relaxed and in alignment, and the shoulder girdle in neutral (not rounded either forward or back). Rest your head on your arm to keep in line with the spine.

4 STEP FOUR

Inhale, engaging the pelvic floor muscles and TVA. Keeping the toes pointed, slowly lift the leg up from the hip to a maximum of 25 degrees. Lengthen through the toes, as if reaching for a light switch.

5 STEP FIVE

Exhale, and at the top of the movement draw the toes toward you as you lower the leg back to the start position, lengthening through the heel as if pressing the foot into a stirrup.

6 STEP SIX

Repeat the movement five times, keeping the leg and foot movement flowing—do not pause at the top or bottom of the movement—then turn over and work the other leg. Gradually increase the repetitions to a maximum of ten.

circles

This movement is an excellent way to finish the leg series exercises. As with the previous exercises, the center needs to be really strong as the base of support is limited and the body will be inclined either to roll forward or rock back. Make sure you are drawing the circles from your hip, not simply wiggling your foot or toes.

Aim: To work the hips, buttocks, and thighs, and promote hip mobility.

Benefits: Transversus abdominus and hip mobility.

1 **STEP ONE**

Lie on your side, with your hips stacked one on top of the other and your legs together with the inner thigh connected. Extend your lower arm, palm up, so that you are in a straight line from your fingertips to your toes.

2 **STEP TWO**

Now angle your legs forward slightly, without changing the position of your spine, which must still be in a straight line from your head to your tail.

3 **STEP THREE**

From this position, separate the top leg and bring it back in line with your hip joint, hovering at hip height. Point your toes. Keep the knee facing forward in the same direction as the hip—do not let it rotate toward the floor. Bend the upper arm at the elbow with the palm over your stomach, for feedback. Keep the top shoulder relaxed and in alignment, and the shoulder girdle in neutral (not rounded either forward or back). Rest your head on your arm to keep in line with the spine.

4 **STEP FOUR**

Inhale, wide and full, engaging the pelvic floor muscles and TVA.

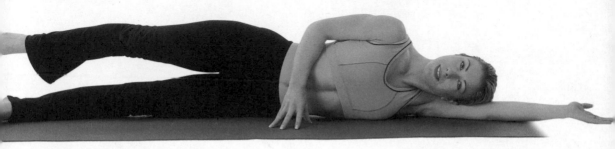

5 **STEP FIVE**

Exhale, and draw circles with your leg—five to the front and five backwards. Keep the circles small—imagine that your leg is inside a small jar, and that you are working around the circumference of the jar. Repeat the movement five times, then turn over and work the other leg. Gradually increase the repetitions to a maximum of ten.

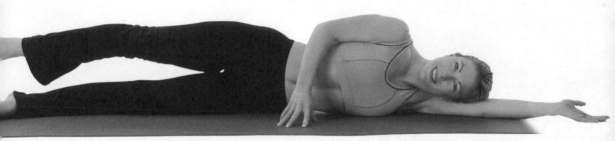

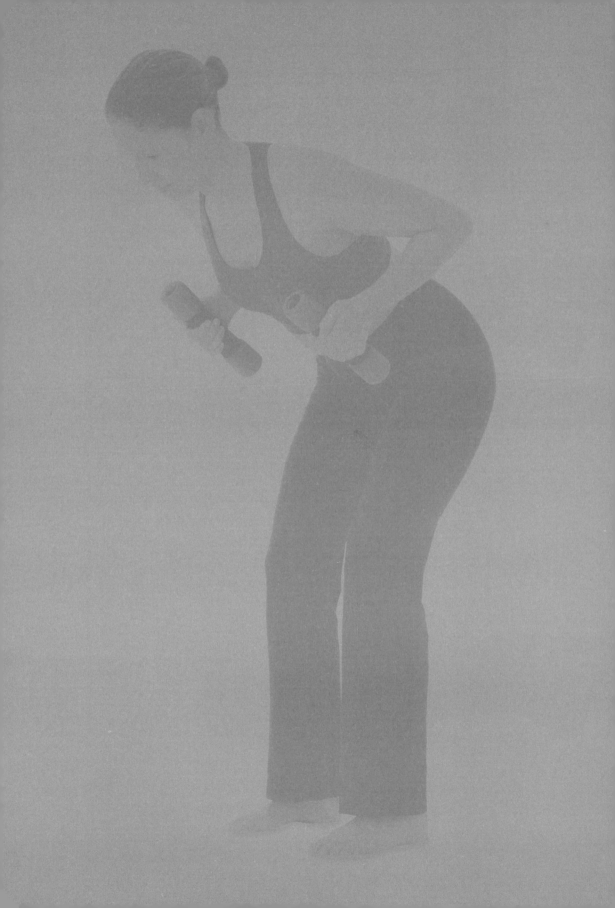

advanced
pilates

introduction

This small batch of advanced level exercises really is quite challenging, but you have been very well prepared for them in the earlier levels, so think positively—you can do it! Do not move on to these until you feel really confident that you are ready, however, and when you do, approach them in exactly the same way as before. Make slow but steady progress and focus all your attention on each movement. There is a lot going on here, so you will need all your concentration, as well as controlled, rhythmic breathing.

For the leg exercises, your base of support is now very limited—whereas in earlier levels you have had the lower leg bent to help hold you in place, here the leg is only slightly angled. This means that if your shoulders and pelvis are not maintained in the neutral position, and your central core is not strong and stable, you are very likely to tip backward or forward. You are also incorporating a side bend into the movement, so you need to be careful not to let the ribs sink or collapse towards the floor. Resting your fingertips very lightly on the floor will give you excellent feedback—as soon as you feel any pressure on them, it is an indication that you are not holding

the essential strong line through the body from pelvis to shoulder.

There are two advanced arm exercises in this section, for working the biceps and triceps—great for toning up flab. As with the leg exercises, it is important that you really control the movement of the arms—do not swing them up and down wildly, but imagine instead that you are working against flowing water, offering that gentle resistance. The movements are more effective if you add weight, either by wearing proper hand weights on your wrists, or by holding a can of soup or beans in each hand—just make sure the contents are the same weight.

This section includes the ultimate Pilates move—the Advanced One Hundred, which pulls together the abdominal exercises, the Lumbar Roll and the Knee Folds, along with superb breath control. You will have a great sense of achievement when you can do this exercise, because it is very demanding of every part of the body but most particularly of the central core which must be 100% stable to support you to a count of ten as you flex the upper body and extend both legs towards the ceiling without any shuddering or loss of form or breath control.

Sounds out of your reach? Of course not! You will get there, although it may take some time unless you were already very fit to start with, and even then you may have to rationalize some of your earlier training. But just imagine—when you can do this exercise, you really will be ready to take on the world! Just keep those Pilates principles in mind—breathing, control and concentration, precision, relaxation and alignment, motivation and visualization—and do the best that you can.

side bicycle

The leg exercises in the earlier sections can be made more advanced by adopting this side bend position of the body. It is very important that when you are in the side bend position, you do not let the ribs sink or collapse to the floor. Keep the ribs connected to a strong centre, so that your body is strong from the pelvis to the shoulder.

Aim: To strengthen and mobilise the hips, and work the buttocks and hamstrings.

Benefits: The hips, gluteus maximus, and hamstrings.

1 STEP ONE
Lie on your side, with your hips stacked one on top of the other and your legs together with the inner thigh connected. Extend your lower arm, palm up, so that you are in a straight line from your fingertips to your toes. Keep your head in line with your spine, with your chin forward.

2 STEP TWO
Inhale, and as you do so place the palm of your upper hand on the floor to aid in pressing you up.

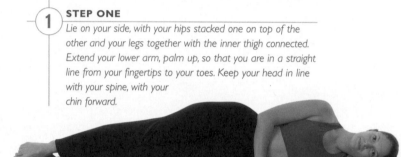

3 STEP THREE
Exhale, and draw your lower arm in toward your body, placing the elbow directly under your shoulder and the forearm on its side, with the fingers pointed away from the body. Keep the top shoulder in neutral, and rest the arm across the navel with the hand (or fingertips as you become more proficient) on the floor for balance.

4 STEP FOUR
Now angle your legs forward slightly, without changing the position of your spine, which must still be in a straight line from your head to your tail.

5 STEP FIVE
From this position, separate the top leg and bring it back in line with your hip joint, hovering at hip height. Point your toes. Keep the knee facing forward in the same direction as the hip—do not let it rotate toward the floor.

6 | STEP SIX

With the top leg hovering at hip height, inhale as you bend the working leg back with the heel toward your buttocks, and then extend the leg forward with the knee at 90 degrees.

7 | STEP SEVEN

Repeat the movement five times, keeping the leg and foot movement flowing—do not pause. Keep the centre connected, as the body will tend to rock forward with the weight of the extended leg.

8 | STEP EIGHT

Turn over and work the other leg, repeating the movement five times. Gradually increase the repetitions to a maximum of ten on each leg.

inner thigh lift

As you carry out this movement, do not just lift the leg up and down—really feel the inner thigh muscle working from the knee to the pubic bone, as if you were resisting gravity. As in the previous exercise, do not let the ribs sink or collapse to the floor. Keep the ribs connected to a strong center, so that your body is strong from the pelvis to the shoulder.

Aim: To stretch and strengthen the inner and outer thighs.

Benefits: The abdominals and the inner and outer thighs.

1 STEP ONE
Lie on your side, with your hips stacked one on top of the other and your legs together with the inner thigh connected. Extend your lower arm, palm up, so that you are in a straight line from your fingertips to your toes. Keep your head in line with your spine, with your chin forward.

2 STEP TWO
Inhale, and as you do so place the palm of your lower hand on the floor to aid in pressing you up.

3 STEP THREE
Exhale, and draw your lower arm in toward your body, placing the elbow directly under your shoulder and the forearm on its side, with the fingers pointed away from the body. Keep the top shoulder in neutral, and rest the palm of the upper hand across the navel for feedback.

4 STEP FOUR
Now angle your legs forward slightly, without changing the position of your spine, which must still be in a straight line from your head to your tail.

5 STEP FIVE
From this position, separate the top leg and bring it back in line with your hip joint.

Bend the top leg at the knee into a figure 4.

...hen place the foot on the floor ...n front of the bottom leg, with ...he bottom leg fully extended.

6 STEP SIX
Inhale and lift up the bottom leg, keeping the leg straight but without locking the knee.

7 STEP SEVEN
Exhale and lower the leg without touching the floor.

8 STEP EIGHT
Repeat the movement five times, without touching the floor between repetitions.

9 STEP NINE
Turn over and work the other leg, repeating the movement five times. Gradually increase the number of repetitions to a maximum of ten on each side.

bicep curl

This exercise is for toning the upper arm to the front. The action is rather like raising the lower arm from a hinge at the elbow. For this exercise and the following one, you will need either small hand weights or two food cans of equal weight—baked beans, for example.

Aim: To work the muscle at the top of the upper arm, which flexes your arm toward your body.

Benefits: The biceps muscle.

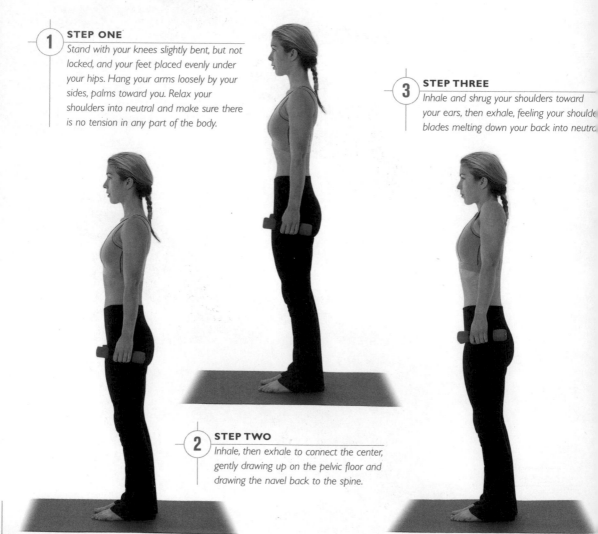

① STEP ONE
Stand with your knees slightly bent, but not locked, and your feet placed evenly under your hips. Hang your arms loosely by your sides, palms toward you. Relax your shoulders into neutral and make sure there is no tension in any part of the body.

③ STEP THREE
Inhale and shrug your shoulders toward your ears, then exhale, feeling your shoulder blades melting down your back into neutra

② STEP TWO
Inhale, then exhale to connect the center, gently drawing up on the pelvic floor and drawing the navel back to the spine.

4 **STEP FOUR**
Inhale.

5 **STEP FIVE**
Exhale and start to curl your arms at the elbows toward your body. As the lower arms move upwards, twist them so that the palms are now facing your body. At the top of the movement, your forearms will be facing your body with your palms just below the chin.

6 **STEP SIX**
Inhale and lower the arms, twisting them so that the palms are facing your sides at the end of the movement.

7 **STEP SEVEN**
Repeat the movement to make a total of ten.

tricep kick backs

This exercise is for toning the triceps at the back of the upper arm, traditionally a slack muscle in women. Again, the elbow acts as a hinge to take the lower arm away from the body. It is essential that you keep the center connected while you are bending over, to protect the spine.

Aim: To work the muscle at the back of the upper arm, which extends the lower arm.

Benefits: The triceps muscle.

1 STEP ONE

Stand with your knees slightly bent, but not locked, and your feet placed evenly under your hips. Hang your arms loosely by your sides, palms toward you. Relax your shoulders into neutral and make sure there is no tension in any part of the body.

2 **STEP TWO**
Inhale, then exhale to connect the center, gently drawing up on the pelvic floor and drawing the navel back to the spine.

3 **STEP THREE**
Maintaining the center connection, hinge forward from the hips. Keeping your spine in alignment, with the knees slightly bent, draw up your elbows like chicken wings. Inhale.

4 **STEP FOUR**
Exhale, engaging the pelvic floor muscles and TVA. Kick back your hands from the elbows, keeping the upper arms in place by your sides.

5 **STEP FIVE**
Inhale and return to the chicken wing position. Repeat the movement to make a total of ten.

advanced one hundred

This is the ultimate Pilates exercise, for which all earlier movements have prepared you. Your central stability must be 100% for this, so you will need all the core and lower abdominal strength gained from previous exercises such as Abdominals 1 and 2, Lower Abdominals, Lumbar Roll and Knee Folds. You must have the pelvis in neutral when performing this exercise, and the shoulder girdle set, and your back must not be flattened or arched out of its natural curves.

1 **STEP ONE**
Lie on your back, with your knees at 45 degrees and your feet in line with your knees. Rest your arms by your sides, palms down.

2 **STEP TWO**
Inhale, lengthening through the body and feeling relaxed.

3 **STEP THREE**
Exhale, connecting the pelvic floor and drawing the navel back to the spine.

4 **STEP FOUR**
Inhale.

5 **STEP FIVE**
Exhale, maintaining the connection with the center, and raise the right leg to 90 degrees.

6 **STEP SIX**
Inhale, maintaining the connection with the leg at 90 degrees.

7 **STEP SEVEN**
Exhale, reinforce the connection with the center, and raise the left leg to 90 degrees.

8 **STEP EIGHT**
Inhale.

9 **STEP NINE**
Exhale, flexing the upper body forward with the arms extended from the shoulders and hovering above the floor. Keep the shoulder girdle in neutral with no tension. Both upper and lower body are now flexed toward the center.

10 **STEP TEN**
Fully extend the legs toward the ceiling. Inhale for a count of five and maintain the position—do not let the upper body release back to the floor. Exhale for a count of five, maintaining the connection to the center.

11 **STEP ELEVEN**
Maintain the position as you continue to breathe, inhaling for a count of five and exhaling for a count of five each time. Aim to repeat the exercise ten times, without losing form—ten repetitions by ten breaths makes the Pilates One Hundred.

single leg stretch with obliques

As with the One Hundred, you must have the pelvis in neutral when performing this exercise, and the shoulder girdle set, and your back must not be flattened or arched out of its natural curves. Good stability at the center is essential as you are aiming for a controlled, deliberate twist using the oblique muscles, without rocking from side to side. Keep your elbows open as you perform the move, and do not be tempted to bring them in toward your head.

Aim: To stabilise the pelvis, strengthen the obliques and lower abdominals, and mobilize the hips.

Benefits: Transversus abdominus, hip flexors/extensors, and obliques.

1 STEP ONE
Lie on your back, with your knees at 45 degrees and your feet in line with your knees. Rest your arms by your sides, palms down.

2 STEP TWO
Inhale, lengthening through the body and feeling relaxed.

3 STEP THREE
Exhale, connecting the pelvic floor and drawing the navel back to the spine.

4 STEP FOUR
Inhale.

5 STEP FIVE
Exhale and let one knee float slowly up toward the ceiling, as if being pulled by an invisible string. Stop when the knee is in line with the hip and the angle of the knee is 90 degrees.

6 STEP SIX
Inhale, maintaining 30% TVA activation and keeping the leg bent at 90 degrees.

7 STEP SEVEN
Exhale, reinforce the connection with the center, and raise the other knee to 90 degrees.

8 STEP EIGHT
Inhale.

9 **STEP NINE**

Exhale, flexing the upper body forward with the arms extended from the shoulders and hovering above the floor. Keep the shoulder girdle in neutral with no tension. Both upper and lower body are now flexed toward the center.

10 **STEP TEN**

Bring your hands to the sides of your head but keep your elbows open. Inhale, to prepare.

11 **STEP ELEVEN**

Exhale, extend your right leg away from the center, and twist at the waist to take your right shoulder to the left knee.

12 **STEP TWELVE**

Inhale and return body and leg to the center.

13 **STEP THIRTEEN**

Exhale, extend your left leg away from the center, and twist at the waist to take your left shoulder to the right knee. Repeat the exercise five times, gradually increasing to a maximum of ten.

glossary

Abdominals The muscles around the spine in the lower back that initiate movement and support and maintain good posture.

Abdominal hollowing Engaging the abdominal muscles so that the abdomen can support and maintain easy, flowing movement.

Alignment Balancing the body so that the weight is distributed evenly over both feet and the skeleton maintains its natural alignment.

Breathing Correct breathing is essential in Pilates, and it is very important to follow the inhale/exhale directions.

Center The area around the middle of the body, which must be strong and stable to initiate flowing movement.

Cervical spine The bones at the top of the spine where it joins the head, more usually referred to as the neck.

Control Controlled movements are essential in Pilates to ensure that each movement is flowing and graceful.

Core Another name for the center of the body, from which good posture and all movement stems.

Core conditioning Working on the muscles at the center or core of the body to promote optimum strength and stability.

Dorsiflex To flex the foot at the ankle so that the toes point forward and th back of the leg is stretched.

Feedback The exchange of information between mind and body that takes place during exercise to ensure that movements are correctly carried out.

Flowing movement Taking one movement into the next in a natural, flowing way, without any hesitation or jerky action.

Gaze In Pilates, it is important to keep your gaze on the horizon to help maintain a good body position.

Girdle of strength The term used to describe the center or core of the body which the Pilates technique aim to strengthen and stabilize to promot flowing movement and good posture

Lumbar multifidus One of the muscles in the center that works with the transversus abdomius to promote easy movement and good posture.

Modification A suggestion for changing a move to make it a little easier until full strength and stability have been achieved in the center.

Motivation Keeping in mind the reason for practicing Pilates, for example, to overcome physical ailments or to promote a feeling of well being.

Neutral In Pilates, this means relaxing the shoulder girdle, spine, and pelvis into their natural positions, so that they are not forced or tilted either to left or right, or forward or backward.

Pail handle The Pilates breath expands the diaphragm and pushes out the ribcage, like a pail handle being lifted up and out.

Pelvis The bones supporting the torso at the base, to which the spine and legs are attached. The pelvic floor muscles support the abdominal muscles to promote movement.

Posture The position in which the body is held. Poor posture can lead to a variety of ailments, and Pilates aims to eliminate this by improving posture.

Precision It is important to carry out Pilates movements with precision – that is, exactly as they are described in the step-by-step directions.

Plantarflex To stretch the foot at the ankle so that the toes point straight out, in alignment with the leg.

Progression A suggestion for changing a move to make it more difficult once full strength and stability have been achieved in the center.

Shoulder girdle The group of bones that make up the shoulders, including the shoulder blades, collar bones, and upper arm bones.

Spine The column of bones, running from the base of the head to the tail of the torso, which connects and supports the skeletal system.

Transversus abdominus The deep postural muscle found in the center of the body, which is key to promoting flowing movement and good posture.

Visualization Creating and maintaining a clear picture of the desired outcome of any activity.

index

index